CW00370348

The Bible Speaks to Me

The Bible Speaks to Me!

Chris Gidney

Marshall Pickering
An Imprint of HarperCollins*Publishers*

Marshall Pickering is an Imprint of
HarperCollins*Religious*
Part of HarperCollins*Publishers*
77-85 Fulham Palace Road, London W6 8JB

First published in Great Britain in 1998 by Marshall Pickering

1 3 5 7 9 10 8 6 4 2

Copyright © 1998 Chris Gidney

Chris Gidney asserts the moral right to be
identified as the author of this work.

A catalogue record for this book
is available from the British Library.

ISBN 0 551 03146 8

Printed and bound in Great Britain by
Caledonian International Book Manufacturing Ltd, Glasgow

CONDITIONS OF SALE
This book is sold subject to the condition that it
shall not, by way of trade or otherwise, be lent, re-sold,
hired out or otherwise circulated without the publisher's
prior consent in any form of binding or cover other
than that in which it is published and without a
similar condition including this condition being
imposed on the subsequent purchaser.

All rights reserved. No part of this publication may be
reproduced, stored in a retrieval system, or transmitted,
in any form or by any means, electronic, mechanical,
photocopying, recording or otherwise, without the prior
permission of the publishers.

Contents

Acknowledgements

Writing a book can be a lonely task, and yet I have been surrounded by people who have supported and encouraged me in this project in a myriad of ways. My special thanks go to: my family – Luke, Anna, Ben and my wife Trinity, for their understanding and support; my editor, James Catford, for his friendship and his belief that I would be able to complete this mammoth project; my PA, Sally Goring, for her sacrificial time and the endless telephone calls she has made on my behalf; Jan Korris, for the immense wisdom and guidance she has given me; my Trustees from Christians in Entertainment – Nick, Bill, Glyn, David, Max and especially Dave, who has given me such moral support; Marilyn, for holding the CIE office together while I wrote; Stuart Weir and the Christians in Sport office, for their advice; and finally to all the contributors, who put their time, thought and energy into choosing their favourite Bible verses.

Especially, I would like to thank God for all the inspiration he has given me while I have been writing and compiling this book. I'm trusting that most of what I have written has come from him, but I know he understands us deeply, and is always able to use even our feeblest efforts. Thank you, Lord.

Letter from an Artiste!

I want to say a very big 'Thank you' to all the actors, sports people and performers who have shared deeply and honestly about their faith and have taken part in this project because they believed it was important.

I have the privilege of knowing personally most of the people who have contributed to this book, some of them as friends. I appreciate their great patience with me as I chased them, sometimes around the world, for their favourite Bible verse!

This is particularly true of the intrepid explorer, Rick Wakeman, whose letter put me in fits of laughter that lasted for days! Here it is:

29th September 1997

Dear Mr Kidney

First of all, I sincerely apologise for the late delivery of my favourite Bible verse. I have no real excuse, but if you would like one, then please choose one of the following:

1. I gave my Bible to a passing Afghan refugee and subsequently couldn't remember exactly where my favourite verse came from.
2. The dog ate my Bible and, by the time it had reappeared through 'natural events', the book of Job, which contains my favourite reading, was missing.
3. Whilst preaching in the jungle of Malaysia last Friday, I was attacked by a Bible-eating tiger and, in order to save my life, I let him eat my Bible.
4. The vicar borrowed it last Sunday and won't give it back.
5. I got my Bible out and had just turned to the page containing my chosen reading, when my youngest son, Oscar, came rushing through the door with his conjuring set. Our dog jumped out from under the table and Oscar tripped over him, sending his conjuring set flying into the air. The box split open, breaking a bottle of vanishing liquid, which spilled all over the pages where my Bible lay open, and within two minutes all the words had vanished.

Yours sincerely
Rick Wakeman

Introduction

I was never any good at remembering where a Bible verse came from, but I am very good at remembering the verse itself. This is because I have found myself relying on what the Bible says more and more in my life. We remember what we experience.

I am a pastor with Christians in Entertainment, and I spend much of my time visiting those who work in show business, who often feel lonely and isolated. I joke about running a spiritual 'meals on wheels' service, but that is what it feels like at times.

There is a lot of spiritual hunger in the entertainment business these days. Lots of performers are asking questions about life, and with more and more household names becoming Christians, it's easier for others to take a closer look at the Christian faith.

Reading the Bible sometimes seems so hard, or even boring and irrelevant to our everyday lives. It can seem like facing a meal that we know will have no taste. It does depend on how the meal is prepared, of course. When we eat a normal meal, we have several choices to make. We can order a takeaway, or have a sandwich at home, or have a meal in a restaurant somewhere. So it is with the Bible. We can dip into the Bible for a quick glance and let it 'fill a gap' like a snack; or we can let others deliver a verse to us, like a take-away; or we can go to church and have a spiritual feast.

Or we can cook at home. With all the convenience food and freezer meals these days, we are in danger of losing the ability to cook for ourselves. My wife Trinity and I love cooking. And eating! We enjoy discovering all the different types of food you can cook, we learn to appreciate all the different tastes and fragrances, and it brings us together as we enjoy the end result in some close moments over a candle-lit dinner.

So it is with the Bible. Instead of totally relying on others for all your spiritual food, why not prepare some for yourself? Dig out your Bible, and instead of having a snack, cook a good meal. There is much you will discover, it will bring you much fulfilment and understanding, and will draw you closer to God. The Bible itself says 'Taste and see that the Lord is good' (Psalm 34:8 NIV)! You'll see that, far from being tasteless and bland, it's actually so full of life that it will make your spiritual taste buds tingle!

'Well, that's all very well, ' you may say. 'I just haven't got the time! And anyway, where would I start?' That's what this book is all about. For older Christians, it's a book that will give a new angle on some Bible verses through the experiences of some people in the public eye. For newer Christians, or for people who are searching for faith it is an excellent place to start looking at the Bible for yourself in a new and easy way.

The 31 chapters have been designed to give an entire month's readings, one for each day. You don't have to do them consecutively, and you can read them more than once. You could even choose one verse and meditate on it for a week, so that you can really digest it properly.

The people who have contributed to this book have all found that the Bible speaks to them. To be more correct, it's actually God who speaks to them, through the Bible. But can we trust the Bible anyway? The following section, 'The Bible – the Facts', shows why I believe we can.

I set the contributors to this book an almost impossible task: to choose only one Bible verse. (Try choosing your own favourite verse and writing it on the inside back cover as a reminder.) Amazingly, only one verse was chosen twice. It really is difficult to choose just one favourite verse from the Bible. It's a bit like singing one line of a song. You don't really get the message of the song, you don't get a sense of the tune, the pace and the atmosphere which the writer intended, and so the line can be taken out of context and made to mean something else. We are sometimes in danger of doing the same kind of thing with our Bibles. So let the verse speak for itself, but look it up in your own Bible too, and read the verses on either side of it.

'Stars', 'names', 'famous', 'prominent', 'celebrities', 'notable' – these are all words which we use to describe the people whom we see on our TVs, listen to on our radios and read about in the newspapers, but are they really any different to you and me? No, not really. They experience the same worries, difficulties, tragedies and joys as anyone else, but sometimes life can be harder for them because we, the public, expect so much from them.

Being in the public eye, for example, means that if you make a mistake it's likely to be splashed across the world's press for all to see and judge. You and I can make our mistakes in private. When we feel low, depressed or upset, we can be just that. Living in the public eye means that while carrying your hurt, you must still go out there and make people laugh, sing with your best voice, do an excellent interview or play your best game. These people are not special – they are just like you and me – but they often have very different needs.

This book contains some of the most honest admissions that I have ever seen written by a group of people who can easily stay behind a mask. Here, the mask is removed because they have all experienced the fact that God knows and loves them without their masks, as he loves all of us as we really are, and not as we would like to be. So, why not join us, take off your own mask, enjoy a spiritual meal and expect the Bible to speak to you!

All of the biblical quotations in this book are taken from the Good News Bible, except for a few from the New International Version, indicated thus: 'NIV'.

The Bible – the Facts

When in the 1970s John Lennon made his famous statement that the Beatles were more popular than Jesus Christ, one can only assume that he was misguided and ill informed. The Holy Bible is still the most popular book in the world, and is still the biggest seller.

The central character of the Bible is Jesus, and the Christian faith is all about him. If it is true that Jesus Christ was the Son of God, and rose again after his death, then we had all better sit up and take notice! If it is not true, then it must be the biggest and cleverest con-trick in the history of our world. But is it worth taking the risk of not checking the facts? I don't think we have a choice. We have a duty to examine the Bible's claims for ourselves. Then we will be in the right position to make our own decision.

There is a lot of confusion about the Bible, though. So here are some straightforward facts, figures and questions that I am often asked.

WHAT IS THE BIBLE?

The Bible is presented in two sections: the Old Testament and the New Testament. The Old Testament was written before Jesus was born and the New was written after he died. The Bible contains 66 different books written by many different people.

HOW CAN WE TRUST THE BIBLE?

Many scholars have set out to discredit and destroy what the Bible has to say, but no one has ever been able to disprove the Bible in any way. The most famous attempt was made by the dogmatic atheist and professional lawyer Josh McDowell, who purposely set out to prove in a court of law that the Bible was inaccurate and not to be trusted. The result was that as Josh dug and delved into every conceivable aspect of the book, he became so convinced of its truth that he became a practising Christian himself. He now specializes in books which give an accurate lawyer's interpretation of Scripture and the Christian faith.

DOESN'T THE BIBLE CONTRADICT ITSELF?

Whenever someone asks me this question, I always ask them to point out where the Bible contradicts itself, promising that I will find an answer. Actually the answer is 'No', the Bible never contradicts itself. It is possible to take verses out of context and prove almost anything, but the important thing is that the Bible should be seen and read as a whole. Considering that the Bible was written by many writers over many hundreds of years, it's actually rather amazing that it 'agrees' entirely with itself from cover to cover! For me, this again confirms that the Bible is God's Word.

WHAT'S THE POINT OF IT, ANYWAY?

The Bible is written as a very practical book. For me, the Bible is God's written recipe for my life. I love cooking, and when I talk to children about Christianity I often show them how to bake a cake. One child reads out the recipe but – silly me! – I get it all wrong. Instead of flour, in goes a flower. Instead of nuts, in go nuts and bolts. Basically, by putting in all the wrong ingredients, I end up with a wonderful mess.

So it is with you and me. We can choose to follow God's recipe and put into our lives all the ingredients that the Maker recommends, or we can put in any old ingredient that feels good at the time. We have all seen the mess that some people make of their lives. As for me, I try to follow God's recipe, but I am aware that I often slip in a wrong ingredient from time to time. Thankfully, the Master Cook is always on hand to help me out!

WHAT IS THE MOST READ BOOK OF THE BIBLE?

Well, probably the Psalms. I love the Psalms because they are so honest. Someone once said that looking into the Psalms is like looking into a mirror. You get a picture of what you really look like! When you read the Psalms you see what you are like inside. It's really helpful sometimes to know that you're not the only one who is in a mess!

CAN THE BIBLE TALK TO ME?

Oh yes! That's the whole point of this book. The Bible is the main way that God is able to talk to us. Everything we do in our lives and everything we do in our churches must be tested against the Scriptures. If you want God to talk to you, read the Bible. Be careful, though. Don't use God's Word as some sort of almanac or horoscope for your future. You can't expect to ask God a question, open your Bible at random and read the first thing you see as an answer to your question. You must read the Bible continuously, asking God to inspire you by his Holy Spirit so that you can understand what the Bible is saying to you as an individual. Don't use the Bible as an insurance policy, but use it as a means of bringing yourself into a closer relationship with God. That's what he wants more than anything.

1

Kriss Akabusi MBE

He's a soldier, public speaker, student, TV star, performer and even a preacher! He's also known as probably the best and nastiest 'baddie' in pantomime. But it was in 1990 that Kriss Akabusi had his greatest individual triumph.

Winning a Gold Medal in the European Athletics Championships was the unbelievable dream come true for Kriss, particularly as he also beat David Hemery's British record, which had remained unsurpassed for 22 years! Kriss went on to win a gold medal once more at the 1991 Tokyo relay event, and a string of other major achievements followed as he represented Britain around the world.

However, despite the highs and lows of an incredibly successful career, the most significant event of Kriss's life was becoming a Christian. It was 1986 and Kriss was at the Commonwealth Games in Edinburgh. Even though it's hard to imagine someone with such a larger-than-life personality ever feeling low, Kriss had known many difficult times in his life. At a very young age he had been abandoned in England by his Nigerian parents when they had to return to their country, which was at war. Kriss spent the next few years of his life moving from one foster parent to another, before finding himself in a children's home in Enfield, North London. He was just eight years old.

Sitting in his hotel room and facing some difficult decisions about his career, Kriss also began to think about his personal life. He had lived in the fast lane for many years, but now he was married and had two daughters, and his life and career needed a new direction. Kriss had not thought about God that often, but holding the special Good News Bible he had been given heightened the pangs of spiritual hunger that he had recently been feeling.

Reading through the whole Bible during those weeks in Scotland, Kriss found in it a new meaning and an outlook on life that was to change him for ever. Soon afterwards, while he was training in America, Kriss simply asked Jesus that if he was there, to come and say 'Hi' to him. Jesus did, and Kriss felt the incredible closeness of God for himself.

In *Winning is not Enough*, Christians in Sport's excellent compilation of the biographies of sports personalities, Kriss is the first one to admit that becoming a Christian didn't solve all his problems – in fact it actually created some new ones! Monica, Kriss's wife, does not share his faith, and feels angry that Kriss is often 'used' by Christians as a celebrity. Learning to cope with the adulation of athletics fans is one thing, but seeing your husband become a Christian 'superstar' is quite another.

However, Kriss is not the sort of character to shy away from all the difficulties that life throws at him, and he knows that in every situation God will be there for him, helping him to overcome each and every hurdle.

KRISS'S FAVOURITE BIBLE VERSES

O Lord, Our Lord,
your greatness is seen in all the world!
Your praise reaches up to the heavens …
When I look at the sky,
which you have made,
at the moon and the stars, which you set in their places –
what is man, that you think of him;
mere man, that you care for him?

Psalm 8:1–4

'I'm sure you can't imagine me ever stopping long enough to take a look into the night sky at all the stars in our galaxy. Yet this is exactly what I do when I need a reminder of just how big God is, and who is really in charge.

'I was totally amazed when someone told me recently that the Universe contains millions of galaxies, and that despite all our modern space technology it would still take us several hundred thousand years just to cross the width of our own galaxy, and that our earth is probably more than 4, 000 million years old! Mind boggling stuff!

'By contrast, we can feel just like small pieces of dust, and yet the Bible says that God actually counts the hairs on our heads because he knows us so personally. Why? Because the God who created the magnificence of the heavens is the same God who made you and me. God's name is truly great, and it is incomprehensible that he should be interested in small people like us, but he is. Even in my greatest triumph this thought has always kept me humble.

'Throughout my life I have constantly sought for victory, using the strongest determination to push through every obstacle to win the race and overcome every difficulty. It has not always been easy, therefore, as a Christian to let God have total control, and I'm often eager to sort things out for myself. I have realized over the years, though, that most of the time I can't, and I just have to let go and trust God.

'When faced with doubts about God's ability and concern to deal with my problems, I reach for these verses. In realizing the true vastness of God, my own problems move into perspective and suddenly I realize that my difficulties are indeed manageable for Father God. Another Psalm talks about God's hands flinging stars into space at the creation of his world. His hands are certainly big enough to hold me. His arms are big enough to shield me and his heart is big enough to love me.'

KRISS'S PRAYER

Dear Lord, thank you that your name is truly majestic, and while I don't understand why you should be interested in people like us, I know you are. For that I am truly grateful. Amen.

2

Cannon & Ball

Tommy Cannon and Bobby Ball have been hailed as Britain's Kings of Comedy. It's easy to see why. In a career spanning more than 35 years they have achieved a string of honours that puts them among the 'greats' of show business.

They have become one of Britain's best-known television comedy acts, having their own TV series for 11 years and starring in several Royal Variety Performances. Their shows consistently sell out at all the major theatre venues. Their pantomime run at the world-famous London Palladium took the largest amount of money ever made in one week in British theatre history.

BOBBY BALL'S STORY

However, the glitz and glamour of show business is not always what it seems, and even being the highest-paid double act could not bring real happiness. Bobby explains: 'At the height of our career I could actually have anything I wanted. I had so much money, I couldn't get rid of it fast enough. The problem was that nothing was ever enough. Whatever I had I wanted more of, but it never satisfied me. I became a very proud person, and I would treat people very badly and expect them to jump at my every demand. I was not a nice person to be near at all.'

Bobby began to drink heavily, saw as many women as he could and got into fights as often as possible. 'It was like living with a volcano, ' Bobby's wife Yvonne remembers. 'You never knew when he was going to erupt.'

In the midst of all this, Bobby had been searching for the truth about God for some time. Having looked into many different religions, he started to read his Bible. 'I liked the Old Testament best, and was enthralled by the way they sometimes didn't eat certain things. I even stopped eating bacon sandwiches for two years, despite the fact that I really loved them. What I really felt was very dirty, and I knew I needed forgiveness.'

Soon after this Bobby contacted Max Wigley, a Theatre Chaplain who had once visited him in his theatre dressing room. 'He explained all about Jesus, and how his death on the cross could enable me not only to be forgiven but actually to start again. I knew it was for me.' Bobby asked Jesus into his life that day, and two months later Yvonne became a Christian too.

TOMMY CANNON'S STORY

When Bobby became a Christian, Tommy noticed a change in his buddy almost immediately. 'I couldn't believe it when he stopped getting drunk, but at first I just put it down to Bobby going through another of his "phases", ' explains Tommy. He remembers walking into Bobby's dressing room one evening and finding himself in the middle of a prayer meeting! He was a bit embarrassed by all this at first, but he knew that Bobby now had something or Someone that he really wanted in his own life.

'Bobby invited me to church one Sunday for a dedication service, and I felt that I couldn't refuse, ' recalls Tommy. 'So I told my wife Hazel and the children to wrap up really warm because it's always cold in churches. When we arrived we couldn't believe how warm and welcoming it was. We had coffee to start with, and the children even had sweets. The service was amazing, with a live band, and a real sense of joy. When we were praying the Pastor asked if anyone wanted to know God in their life, and my hand went up in the air because I knew that this was just what I wanted. To my surprise Hazel's hand was in the air too!'

Since becoming committed Christians Cannon & Ball have continued to break box-office records, some of them during their own highly successful Gospel Tours. Despite suggestions in the media that Tommy became a Christian just because Bobby did, or that they became 'religious' in order to give an uplift to their flagging career, Cannon & Ball are still in demand all over the country, and even continue to receive some of the biggest pantomime box-office advances of their career!

Nor have they been free from all the difficulties of being in the public eye. The newspapers often try to dig up some sort of story from the past, sometimes even trying to disprove their Christian faith. But as Bobby says, 'The career is not as important as our relationship with God. He pulled me out of a pit and set my feet on a rock, and I'll love him for ever for that.'

Bobby and Tommy often enjoy mobile Bible studies while they are travelling together in the car. Bobby reads the Bible while Tommy drives, it's a great double act! Here Bobby picks a favourite verse for them.

TOMMY AND BOBBY'S FAVOURITE BIBLE VERSE

Jesus answered, 'I am telling you the truth: no one can see the Kingdom of God unless he is born again.'

John 3:3

'For me this is the most important aspect of the Christian faith. I realize that it sounds very strange, though. Even the priest Nicodemus, who asked what Jesus meant by this, at first took him literally. What Jesus meant, however, is that when you realize your need for God, you have to stop doing it your way, hand everything over, and start again. It was a revolutionary concept in Jesus's day because it didn't depend on what nationality you were, or who your father was, but on whether you were willing to wholeheartedly ask God to be in control of your life.

'For me, the idea of being "born again" was very important. I was ashamed of my past and wanted God to bury it as deep as possible. In fact I love the bit in the Bible that says that God takes our sins and totally blots them out. God does not remember them any more. That was just what I needed. I wanted to be washed inside and out and to stand before my God as if I was brand new – born again!

'It's important, too, to understand that it's not like deciding that you're going to be good from now on, like a New Year's resolution. People can be God-fearing and church-going and yet not be born again. Someone once said that going to church doesn't make you a Christian any more than going to MacDonald's makes you a hamburger!

'Only God's Holy Spirit can enable us to be born again, and it's still a revolutionary thing today. We are all so used to handling things ourselves, in our way and in our time. Sometimes we are also too proud to let God into our lives. We must learn to "let go and let God". Not just once, when we accept God into our lives, but every single day.'

BOBBY'S PRAYER

Bobby is actually a poet. His chosen prayer is the closing section of a poem he has written called 'Power of Praise':

> *Please forgive me, but I find it hard to apologize,*
> *To be able to see the other person's point of view.*
> *But deep inside, behind all this sinful pride,*
> *I want to be just like you.*
>
> *Really deep in my soul, I want to be sensitive,*
> *I want to open my eyes and see.*
> *I no longer want this pride to be ever consuming,*
> *I want to trade for humility.*

As Jesus said, pride is a sin
And it will eventually bring about a man's fall.
You see, I've been too busy being proud,
I didn't listen to Jesus's call.

If only you could forgive me, Jesus,
For my sins, but most of all my pride.
Forgive, for all the people my proudness hurt,
And for the way to myself I lied.

So fill me, Jesus, with your love,
Fill me to my innermost being.
Take away this mask from my eyes,
Give me joy like a blind man first upon seeing.

Earnestly I beg you, Jesus,
Wash away my sin as only you can,
And turn this arrogant and ignorant thing
Into a brand new, humble man.

3

Russell Boulter

Best known as the character DS Boulton in the popular TV series *The Bill*, Russell actually began his career with the Royal Shakespeare Company in 1985. With an unusual ability to play characters right across the dramatic spectrum, Russell has appeared in classical, musical, comedy and TV productions. His professional theatre credits range from *Hamlet* at the Bristol Old Vic to *Blood Brothers* in London's West End.

On television he has been featured in a whole range of programmes such as *The Darling Buds of May*, *Casualty*, *Heartbeat*, *Luv* and *Brookside*. Russell has also directed some productions, including J. B. Priestley's *They came to a city*.

Married to Jenny, an accomplished artist, Russell lives in London and commutes each day to wherever *The Bill* is being filmed. It may seem like a glamorous lifestyle, but the reality is that filming with the sort of schedules which *The Bill* has can be extremely exhausting. Russell will often arrive on set in the early hours of the morning, he may be transported to several different locations during the day, and he may finish with a 'night shoot', arriving home late, only to get up early again the next day.

There is also a lot of pressure to learn lines very quickly, and when he is not on camera Russell is to be found in a corner somewhere going through the day's script. When you are contracted to a television company, there are times when it seems that you are at the mercy of the programme's Director. You can be called to work at any time, day or night, and this plays havoc with Russell's personal and social life, not to mention his church life!

Russell became a Christian in 1981 at All Souls Church, Langham Place, London, during an invitation service. The preacher was Eric Delve and the title of the sermon was 'Everything you have always wanted to know about God, but were afraid to ask.'

When asked if he feels that acting is an appropriate career for a Christian, Russell says, 'I think the question for the previous generation of Christians who wanted to pursue an acting career was, "Dare I use this talent for God?" The question for my generation is "Dare I *not* use this talent for God?"'

RUSSELL'S FAVOURITE BIBLE VERSES

Ask, and you will receive; seek, and you will find; knock, and the door will be opened to you. For everyone who asks will receive, and anyone who seeks will find, and the door will be opened to him who knocks.

Matthew 7:7–8

'I moved to London in the autumn of 1981. I was 18 years old and I had come to study drama on the three-year acting course at LAMDA.

'There had been 800 applicants for 30 places. As you can imagine, the pressure was on! Despite enjoying my course, I was a long way from home and I didn't know anyone in London, so in my first term I found myself spending a lot of time alone.

'Before I had left, my uncle had given me my first Bible and had suggested that I should read the Gospels. I had a lot of time on my hands and so I did, especially in the evenings. I read them as I would have read a novel and, frankly, I was shocked!

'The Jesus whom I met in the Gospels was radically different from the Jesus I had been told about at school in RE classes. This Jesus was dangerous and exciting. He turned over the money-changers' tables, called religious hypocrites "sons of snakes" and healed the broken-hearted. He was accused of being a drunkard at wedding parties, of hanging out with prostitutes and lepers. He cast out devils, he had authority, he was brave, fearsome and passionate, and I really liked him! This caused me a problem because I considered myself to be an atheist, and the Jesus I liked quite clearly described himself as the Son of God.

'Then I noticed this verse: "Ask, and you will receive." I thought it only fair to take this Jesus at his word, and so I prayed and asked this question: "If you are God and you love us, why do you allow so much suffering and evil? If you are good you would stop it. So maybe you don't exist."

'I didn't expect a reply, but the next day I received a book in the post from my uncle. It was by C. S. Lewis and was entitled *God in the Dock*.

'In it I read his argument that God *does* oppose evil but will not violate our freedom. We are free to love, or to hate. He will not turn us into machines. If we lived as God suggested, then there would be a massive decrease in suffering, as most suffering is caused by human beings. If you don't believe in God and therefore believe that there is no absolute right or wrong and the universe is empty and without meaning, then why is suffering and evil a problem for you anyway? I had to admit that it was a pretty good answer.

'The next morning, walking through central London to drama school, I asked my next question. "How do I know You are really there, and not just in my imagination? Why won't you *say* something to me?"

'As I walked along I felt a suggestion slip into my thoughts: "Look to your left." I did, and I saw a church notice-board on which was a poster. It said, "If you don't understand my silence, how will you understand when I speak?"

'Touché!

'From then on I started to seek out God, although, looking back, I think he was looking for me. I still had a lot of questions. Mostly I was afraid of what God was really like. Did he really care about me? Did he want to annihilate my personality? Was he just playing games with the Universe? If I became a Christian, would my friends reject me?

'What I found was that God was loving, protective and easy to be with. I was offered a relationship in which God treated me with respect. I found a teacher, guide and friend. It was as if he was prepared to move heaven and earth to have a conversation with me, which was more than I deserved. When I had knocked, the door had opened.

'I have found that salvation is a free gift, but it isn't cheap. To receive it you have to give everything you are to the giver. These verses from Matthew still apply to me now. God encourages you to ask him your questions, to seek him out, to knock on his door. So, as my uncle said to me when he gave me a Bible, "Don't let other people tell you what to think. Find out for yourself."

RUSSELL'S PRAYER

Riches I need not, nor man's empty praise;
Thou my inheritance through all of my days;
Thou and Thou only though first in my heart;
High king of heaven, my treasure Thou art.

4

Dora Bryan

Dora Bryan recently celebrated more than 60 years in show business, and is still one of the country's best-loved actresses. She started her career in 1935 at the Palace Theatre in Manchester when she was just 12 years old, and today she still manages to do the same tap dance and splits that she did then!

Although Dora is often seen as one of the funniest ladies on television, her career seems to have spanned every conceivable style in theatre, television and films around the world. By the time Dora was 37 she had featured in 28 films, and for her classic role in *A Taste of Honey* she was awarded the title of Best Actress of the Year in 1961. Her stunning performance in the long-running *Hello Dolly* at the Theatre Royal, Drury Lane, was another highlight in Dora's glittering career. She even had a chart hit with 'All I want for Christmas is a Beatle', appearing on *Top of the Pops* in 1963. The song is still played every Christmas.

However, being a wife and mother is just as important to Dora as being an actress. She married the cricketer Bill Lawton in 1954, and they have one of the longest marriages in show biz. But life has not been easy for them, and they have experienced headaches, heartaches and personal tragedies together. Dora lost three babies through premature birth, but happily she and Bill were able to adopt two children, Daniel and Georgina. Later Dora gave birth to a son, William.

Sadly, when Daniel was just 17 he was diagnosed as having a rare form of arthritis, and Dora and the family had to learn to adjust to the pain and difficulties that this disease caused. Dora herself had to cope with the paralysing depression that was to continually dog her personal life.

In Spain in 1972 the family were involved in a serious accident when their car went over the edge of a sheer drop on a mountain road. Miraculously, every member of the family survived, but the accident brought home to Dora the fragility of life.

Dora's first real encounter with God was when she was asked to play Cliff Richard's mum in the Billy Graham film *Two a Penny*. It was Dora's first step towards the strong Christian faith which she now has. After the filming, sensing that Dora wanted to know more about Christianity, Cliff asked her if she would like to meet a pastor friend of his named Max Wigley. Dora remembers that Max looked more like a rugby player than a vicar when she first met him while she was starring in *Hello Dolly*. Max gave her an easy-to-read Bible (she still has it now, but it's tattered and well marked!).

One day, in between the matinée and the evening performance, Max asked Dora if she would like to know Jesus in a personal way. Dora knelt down on the floor and invited Jesus to come and share her life. She remembers that she saw no flashes of lightning or angels, but she felt a wonderful sense of calm, and she knew that she had taken a big step.

Dora says that her faith and trust in God has got her through the toughest of times. Only recently she endured the pain and tragedy of seeing her adopted daughter Georgina die of alcohol abuse. Despite the difficulties and the many unanswered questions, God has remained at the heart of Dora's life and work.

DORA'S FAVOURITE BIBLE VERSES

I have loved you with an everlasting love; I have drawn you with loving-kindness. I will build you up again and you will be rebuilt.

Jeremiah 31:3–4 NIV

'I'm not very good at regularly reading my Bible. It's often difficult to know where to start, so my daily Bible notes are always helpful. This verse from Jeremiah often reminds me just how much God really loves me and understands me, even more than I understand myself.

'Knowing I am loved by God makes it easy to pray. I am a great believer in prayer, and I pray all the time, whether I'm about to go on stage or doing the washing up. I love talking to God.

'The love that God has for us is everlasting. His love isn't dictated by the way we feel, or what we have or haven't done that day. He loves us no matter where we are or what we are thinking or where we are heading. I'm so glad that in the middle of feeling at my worst, God's love keeps on flowing, reminding me of just how special he thinks I am.

'God also talks about building in this verse. Sometimes I feel that God has had to do a lot of rebuilding in my life, because there has been a lot of difficulty and damage at times. The building he does is often on the inside, though, and I know that I have been able to get through some of the traumas in my life only because God was there with me, healing the pain.

'I still suffer from depression from time to time, but I am confident that God knows how I feel, and why, and his rebuilding programme in me goes on. At the end of the day it's God's total love for me that matters the most.'

DORA'S PRAYER

Dear Lord, thank you for revealing yourself to me. Thank you for all I have, and for teaching me that love is all that matters. Please help me each day to be a good witness for you in this way. Amen.

5

Nina Carter

She was earning more than £1, 000 a day. As one of the UK's top models in the 1970s, Nina Carter appeared in *Vogue*, *Cosmopolitan*, *She* and many other publications worldwide.

Born in Solihull in the West Midlands, Nina remembers being a tearaway even at the age of nine. Family life was comfortable, but as her father was an entrepreneur, he was always changing his job, and by this time Nina had lived in six different homes and had changed school ten times.

On one occasion her father fell while carrying a heavy bag of potatoes. As a result of this he was bedridden for nearly three years with a form of sclerosis. During this time her father arranged for Nina to attend the local Anglican church for confirmation classes. 'Most of it went straight over my head,' admits Nina, 'though I do feel that God somehow became part of me then.'

She hadn't fully realized how ill her father was. One day,

when the family were at his bedside, her mother fainted and Nina's brother carried her mother out. While they were gone, Nina's father died in her arms. She was just 15 years old.

Keen to be the success her father had wanted her to be, she entered a beauty contest and won. Joining the Beauty Queen circuit, she had instant success. She was encouraged to go into glamour modelling because of her short height, and so Nina soon found herself in great demand for Pirelli calendars, swimwear catalogues and TV advertisements. She became famous for appearing in a Martini commercial and many others.

She was soon introduced to the topless girls in the daily newspapers and was one of the first three to be published in this way. It was here that she found she could make £1,000 per day, and her lifestyle became more and more glamorous. 'My mother was actually very embarrassed about what I was doing,' Nina remembers, 'and I began to spend less and less time at home.'

A change in the direction of her career meant working for people like David Bailey and appearing on the front covers of many of the country's top fashion magazines. She enjoyed this prestigious work, but continued to live a luxurious life, even though the money had dropped considerably. With debts starting to mount up, she was encouraged to go into the music business. With some friends she produced a record which became a number-one hit in Japan, and her band 'Blonde on Blonde' played throughout Europe.

Noticing that many of her peers were on drugs, it wasn't long before Nina followed suit. Spending enormous sums of money to maintain her habit, she was suddenly confronted with a serious throat problem which put her in hospital for four months. 'I realized I had to make a break, ' says Nina.

After 15 years of fast living, Nina decided to leave London. She bought a cottage in Surrey and started her own cosmetics business. She travelled around the country giving lectures to women's organizations and groups. It was an enlightening period of her life that eventually brought her face to face with reality.

It was during this time that she met Rick Wakeman, who asked her to sing on one of his albums. She accepted, and when Rick invited her to the launch of the recording in Cannes she flew out to join him. Meeting him at the hotel, she noticed that he looked extremely ill. In fact he had just suffered a heart attack. She helped him up to his hotel room, but then they were accosted by a member of the tabloid press who threatened them, saying that he would give them a week to tell him their story, or he would tell it himself.

Months of press hounding and speculation followed, which had the effect of throwing Nina and Rick closer together. Their feelings for each other grew, and eventually they fell in love and decided to get married.

Since that day life for them has been like a tornado! Nina has two children with Rick, and three stepchildren. It's a very happy and rewarding family, and one where there is never a dull moment.

Nina became a committed Christian at the same time as Rick did. Since she made that commitment her life has changed dramatically, and she feels she has more peace and purpose in her life.

Nina particularly enjoys using all the expertise and experience which she gained as a top model to present her own brand of beauty therapy. Calling her sessions 'Beauty from

Within', Nina travels the country showing women how they can make the most of the individual features which God has given them, while telling them a little about her own life and her journey to faith.

NINA'S FAVOURITE BIBLE VERSES

Lord, you have examined me and you know me.
You know everything I do;
from far away you understand all my thoughts.
You see me, whether I am working or resting;
you know all my actions.
Even before I speak,
you already know what I will say.
You are around me on every side;
you protect me with your power.
Your knowledge of me is too deep;
it is beyond my understanding.

Psalm 139:1–9

I have chosen these verses, out of the many verses that are special to me, because they remind me that, although God is more powerful than we can ever understand, he is also our Father.

Remarkably, he knows every one of us individually, and he knew our future even before we were born. As we live our lives, struggling to make the right decisions, this Psalm reminds us that God is always there beside us. He's in our hearts and in our thoughts, continually turning the pages of our lives, day by day. He is always with us and will love us no matter how many mistakes we make.

Despite the difficulties we encounter, it's always important for me to remain positive about what the Lord is doing in my life, and about how he is using me for his glory and purpose. There has been a lot written about how Rick and I hit rock bottom during our lives, but we both feel that in our case, our journey to Christ had to be dramatic in order for us to listen. Rick and I were both so ambitious and so engrossed in lifestyles that were far away from God that he needed to shout to get our attention. He could do this because, even though we didn't really know him, he knew us. Not only did he know us, but he knew us so intimately. He knew what we were doing, he knew what we were thinking, and he knew what we needed.

NINA'S PRAYER

Heavenly Father,
Thank you for the miracle of life.
Thank you for your enduring and never-ending love.
Thank you for your patience and wisdom.
Help us, Lord, to always bring our days before you,
with the knowledge that, with your powerful hands upon us,
our lives will be blessed.

Forgive us, Lord, for all the times when we are fickle
and are unable to own up to our inadequacies.
Help us to keep our eyes continually fixed on you.
In your holy name we pray. Amen.

6

Johnny Cash

His nickname is The Man in Black. He's also the closest thing the USA has to a living legend. Yet it seems that this major international performer has had more than his fair share of personal tragedies.

Johnny Cash has spent more than four decades in the music business. He's written more than a thousand songs, scored many top hits, written two books, featured in films and appeared on hundreds of TV shows across the world.

Known for his honest, gritty lyrics, J. R. Cash was born in Kingsland, Arkansas, on 26 February 1932. His parents were destitute farmers looking for a better life. For a time they found it, moving to the Mississippi Delta with a government grant to grow a cotton field. Johnny was just three years old at the time. He remembers the long journey in the back of a truck. He recalls one rainy night when he slept in the truck under a tarpaulin. His mother would send him, his two brothers and his two sisters to sleep with the sound of her old Sears-Roebuck guitar. The Gospel songs she sang to them gave Johnny a sense of closeness and comfort that could not be found any other way.

The family settled down to their new way of life and his father bought a battery radio. Johnny loved listening to it. The melodies and songs lifted him far away from the mud and cotton that was the reality of his young life. When his 14-year-old brother Jack was fatally injured in a chainsaw accident it was Johnny's love of the many Southern Gospel songs he had heard on the radio that somehow kept him going.

Johnny's love of music made him determined to learn the guitar for himself, hoping that one day he too might sing on the radio. When Johnny was 12 his mother's guitar had mysteriously disappeared (it was probably sold to buy the family some food), but a school-friend owned an old guitar, and so Johnny went to his friend's house every day after school. Walking the three miles back home in the dark each evening, Johnny always comforted himself by singing those old Gospel tunes.

Before long, Johnny had saved up and bought his own guitar. He and some friends formed an acoustic band called 'The Barbarians'. They would play in the bars and honky-tonks until the places were closed for the night, or they were too drunk to carry on.

In 1954, after a stint in the US Air Force, Johnny moved to Memphis and was determined to make his first record in that famous town. After auditioning for Sam Phillips at Sun Studios, he recorded his debut album, including the classic 'Cry, Cry, Cry' and several other Cash originals.

Johnny met and married June Carter in 1968. He has had a long string of hits including 'A Boy Named Sue', 'I Walk the Line' and 'Ring of Fire', and he has won eight Grammy awards. It has not been success all the way, however, and he has suffered problems with drug and alcohol abuse. Once he was arrested for possession of narcotics, and he spent a night in jail.

But his Christian faith has always seen him through the blackest of times, and his latest album, *Unchained*, expresses his feeling of finding freedom through his deeply rooted faith in a God who loves him and cares for him, and who gave him his most precious gift of all – his music.

JOHNNY'S FAVOURITE BIBLE VERSE

If you live according to your human nature, you are going to die; but if by the Spirit you put to death your sinful actions, you will live.

Romans 8:13

Have you fallen over in the mud today? Do you feel a failure in God's eyes? Are you tempted to give up trying? Well, here's the good news! You're not on your own!

Johnny says that some of the blackest moments of failure in his own life were times when he knew the special comfort and reassurance of the living God. This verse from Romans reminds us that desiring and pursuing things which seem innocent and pleasing can sometimes be extremely harmful. Johnny is highlighting the fact that we live in an age of self-gratification.

He says that this verse 'delivers me from self-destructing thoughts and actions'. What is really fantastic about this verse is that it says we don't have to try and get it right all on our own. When we accept Jesus Christ into the driving-seat of our lives, we have God's Holy Spirit within us to help us and strengthen us through all the everyday trials that we face. It's when we try and do it on our own, thinking that it's best to try and show God how clever we are, that we often come unstuck.

If you really do want God to be in the driving-seat of your life, stop trying to grab the wheel yourself, and trust that he does know what is best. God is interested in every part of our lives, and Johnny's chosen prayer reflects this.

JOHNNY'S PRAYER

Our Father, who is in heaven,
Honoured be your name.
May your kingdom come
And may your will be done
Here on earth like it is in heaven.
Give us this day our daily bread
And forgive our sins,
Helping us to forgive those who have done wrong to us.
Steer us away from temptation
And deliver us from evil.
For yours is the power
And the glory,
For ever and ever. Amen.

7

Steve Chalke

Steve Chalke is not your usual vicar! Not content just to fill the media 'God slots', Steve is a regular presenter on GMTV, Britain's most popular breakfast television programme, where he researches and discusses anything from parenting to bullying, from death to debt. As well as having his own live ITV networked show *Chalke Talk*, he has hosted numerous other programmes, including *The Time, The Place*. He does present religious programmes as well, however, including the BBC's *First Light* and, of course, *Songs of Praise*.

Steve is also a prolific, best-selling author. His most recent book, *How To Succeed As A Parent*, offers help to all those who are struggling with the responsibility of bringing up children. His regular newspaper and magazine columns offer advice for all manner of problems.

His Oasis Trust was founded in 1985 to develop social awareness and to try to meet the needs of disadvantaged young and homeless people throughout the UK. The Trust now has a team of thousands developing social care initiatives, including medical and educational programmes worldwide.

Even though Steve's speaking engagements take him as far afield as the USA, Africa, Australia, India and Europe, he is not the kind to stay in the pulpit for long, but is concerned with actively showing the world just how much God loves every individual.

Steve does have a home life too! He lives in South London with his wife Cornelia and their children, Emily, Daniel and Abigail, and a cat called Friday. His biggest sin is supporting Crystal Palace Football Club!

STEVE'S FAVOURITE BIBLE VERSE

> *The Word became a human being and, full of grace and truth, lived among us. We saw his glory, the glory which he received as the Father's only Son.*

John 1:14

'Without hesitation, I can say that this is the Bible verse that most consistently challenges and inspires me. It describes the kind of person I want to be. As St Augustine said, "Preach the gospel. If necessary, use words." Jesus didn't just "preach the Word of God" – he *was* the Word of God. Everything God wanted to say to humanity was wrapped up in Jesus, who made it transparent for all the world to see.

'As a result, people didn't just say they'd heard about God's glory in Jesus – they could say, "We've *seen* it." I want to be that transparent as well. My goal is for people to be able to see God in me. I want to be someone who lives God's Word, not just through what I say, but through who I am.

'John then goes on to explain that the hallmarks of Jesus's life were "grace and truth". I was brought up in a church where truth was valued very highly. In the words of Tony Campolo, an American pastor, "I was so sound, I believed in the Virgin Birth before I knew what a virgin was." But I've slowly learned that when truth is severed from grace, it becomes nothing more than a burden – the kind of thing the hypocritical Pharisees in the Bible were famous for.

'Grace is the essential ingredient. It's the environment in which truth should always be spoken and in which it can be most easily received. It was grace that allowed Jesus, without having to sacrifice truth, to make friends with the kind of people whom the Church so often chases from its doors. I always want to be a person who is full of the grace of God, as well as a spokesman for his truth.'

STEVE'S PRAYER

Dear Lord, thank you that, in Jesus, we see what you're like. Help me to become the kind of person who, in turn, makes Jesus easy to see. Amen.

Rosemary Conley

It was purely by accident that Rosemary Conley discovered the benefits of her now-famous Hip & Thigh Diet. Having been diagnosed as having gall stones, she was given the option of either surgery or eating less fat. She chose to change her diet, and was amazed at how quickly her body shape was totally transformed, making her look good and feel the best she had ever felt in her life. She then did some extensive research into the effects of the special low-fat diet which she had created for herself. As a result, Rosemary's diet plan, combined with the right kind of exercise, has given new hope to millions of people.

Her book, *The Complete Hip & Thigh Diet*, became an international bestseller in 1988 and remained on the top-selling list for more than nine years, selling in excess of two million copies. Subsequent books and videos have all been instant bestsellers.

Rosemary maintains a high media profile, often appearing on television and radio and writing columns for several magazines and journals. Her own *Diet & Fitness Magazine* was launched in 1996, and with contributions from leading experts in the fields of nutrition, health and fitness, has become one of the most authoritative magazines in its field.

The Rosemary Conley Diet & Fitness Clubs were launched in 1993 across the UK. Operating under a franchise system, carefully selected instructors are fully trained to teach the Rosemary Conley philosophy of fitness. It has become the fastest-growing franchise operation in the UK, with over 2,300 weekly classes throughout the country. Rosemary has worked in the diet and fitness industry for 25 years, and is now established as the market leader in this field.

She lives in Leicestershire with her husband, Mike Rimmington, with whom she runs the Rosemary Conley Group of companies. She has a daughter by her first marriage, and they are all committed Christians. Rosemary's faith has never been an embarrassment to her. Rather, it has helped to shape her fitness philosophy. She believes it is important that people should look after the bodies that God has given them.

ROSEMARY'S FAVOURITE BIBLE VERSES

Love is patient and kind; it is not jealous or conceited or proud; love is not ill-mannered or selfish or irritable; love does not keep a record of wrongs; love is not happy with evil, but is happy with the truth. Love never gives up; and its faith, hope, and patience never fail.

1 Corinthians 13:4–7

'I became a Christian in 1986 when I asked the Lord into my life. I surrendered totally to him, and from that moment on I have tried to live my life his way – not mine!

'There were no blinding flashes of light or cracks of thunder when I asked Jesus into my life, but I know that as soon as I had prayed, kneeling at the side of my bed, something very dramatic had happened. When I awoke the next morning I knew that my sins had been forgiven, and I was reborn and ready to live a new life. I had no idea my life would change so dramatically in the years that followed.

'While I have enjoyed great success with my books, videos, diet and fitness clubs and magazine, none of it could have been achieved without the blessing of the Lord. He gave me the energy, the ideas and the opportunities, and the humility to realize that what I had achieved was God's own gift.

'Since I became a Christian, I have felt the most unbelievable amount of love towards my husband, my daughter and all of my fellow human beings. That is why I have chosen these verses. I know that this is God's love reaching through me to touch others. We cannot survive in this world without love and the feeling that we are loved.

'Amazingly, the more we love others, the more love they give back. Perhaps that is one of the greatest things I have learned since becoming a Christian. I remember at first being very worried that I didn't know how to serve the Lord. Then one day I had a chat with a minister, who assured me that the Lord would tell me in his own good time what he wanted me to do, and so I felt more relaxed. Extraordinarily, as I drove home after that conversation I turned on the car radio, and the next song that was played was Cliff Richard and Sarah

Brightman singing that beautiful song from *Phantom of the Opera*, "All I ask of You". I felt that through the lyrics the Lord was saying to me, "All I ask of you is that you love me." In my mind it was so clear that this was the message that was being given to me, and I was elated because I felt that yes, I could do that easily.

'This was a turning-point for me. Every day I try to remember to tell the Lord, as well as my husband, that I love him. Love is something that we should never take for granted. To know that the Lord Jesus loves us more than we could ever love him should be one of the greatest comforts we will ever experience. It is his love at work through me that enables me to face each day, determined to help others in whatever way he shows me.'

ROSEMARY'S PRAYER

Lord Jesus, thank you for your abounding love, your patience and your forgiveness. You hold no record of wrongs, and I am grateful that you showed me the way to love you. I love you, Lord Jesus, and I ask you to make me the person that you want me to be. Help me, Lord, to be more like you. Help me to serve you in serving others. In your name. Amen.

9

Wendy Craig

She is everybody's favourite TV Mum, starring in such classic series as *Not in Front of the Children*, *And Mother Makes Three*, *And Mother Makes Five* and the much-acclaimed *Butterflies*.

In real life, Wendy Craig is not the dithering and flustered character seen on television, but is a very clever and accomplished actress. The BBC's peak-hour drama series *Nanny* was based on her own idea, and she wrote many of the episodes of *And Mother Makes Five* herself.

Wendy's professional biography is phenomenal, and a list of her awards gives an idea of the amount of love and esteem which people inside and outside of her profession have for her. Since she has been 'Actress of the Year', 'BBC Personality of the Year' and 'BBC TV's Woman of the Year', it is no great surprise that she was also voted 'Funniest Woman on Television'.

Indeed, her many awards reflect the scope of her work right across the spectrum of entertainment, from films and television to the stage and even books and albums. Wendy won a gold disc for her recorded version of *The Tales of Beatrix Potter*, and her *Busy Mum's* cook books have been bestsellers. She is also an actress who can play almost any role, from classic parts to pantomime, and she was once described as 'One of the six best young actresses in the Western world'.

Yet despite all this accolade, it would be difficult to find a more humble actress. She often lacks confidence, and her doubts about her own ability only serve to enhance her humility and grace. Her deep faith in God and her steady reliance on him are obviously central in her life. Wendy is someone who knows her worth, and yet is able to see that God is much bigger than she is.

She is the widow of the musician and journalist Jack Bentley, to whom she was married for 39 years. She has two sons – Alaster, an oboist with the Birmingham Royal Ballet, and Ross, a writer.

Wendy's Christian faith began when she was a child, when her grandmother taught her all about Jesus. However, as she got older she began to drift away from her beliefs. It was a personal tragedy that caused Wendy to return to her childhood faith, finding that it now had even more relevance than before. Wendy knew that getting back to the security of God's love was the only way to put everything right. She has since recognized that this was the most important and life-changing decision she has ever made.

WENDY'S FAVOURITE BIBLE VERSE

The Lord your God is with you;
his power gives you victory.
The Lord will take delight in you,
and in his love he will give you new life.
He will sing and be joyful over you.

Zephaniah 3:17

'When asked to choose a favourite verse from the Bible I thought, "How can I do that? There are so many verses which speak to me. How can I possibly choose just one?" I thought of the hundreds of times when I'd been strengthened, guided and enlightened by God's Word in different situations. To choose just one verse was an awesome task!

'However, realizing that I had been asked to contribute because I am a Christian working in the entertainment industry helped me to focus my thoughts. I managed to whittle my choice down to several verses which have helped me when preparing for a performance. Finally, I decided on the above verse from Zephaniah, an Old Testament prophet.

'In common with a lot of actors, I am not the most confident person in the world. I am so often filled with doubt – doubt of every kind, including self-doubt, as well as doubt about my faith. Many times I have stood in the wings, at the side of the stage, before making my entrance, filled with terror and convinced that I'd never get through the show.

'Many times while praying, I've suddenly caught my breath with the thought, "Is God really there? Does he really listen to me, or am I just deluding myself?"

'I've often sensed my own inadequacy and felt my confidence ebbing away. I'm sure that this must sound impossible to those who see me exuding confidence and energy when I'm on the television or on stage, but this is the truth.

'Isn't it a wonderful thing, then, that the Scriptures always have a word to help us if we care to look? When I came across my chosen verse, it leaped out at me. It was just what I needed to hear at that moment. Here was the reassurance I was seeking.

'Imagine God taking delight in me – yes, me, with my flat feet and squeaky voice! He wanted to wrap me in his love and quieten my fears. He was happy with me and sang with joy over me and, best of all, he wanted to save me – to save me from myself through his grace, so mysterious and desirable. What proof had I that he would do all this? His Word is proof enough for me. I knew that God does not make rash promises, and therefore I knew I could trust him.

'When you discover that you are loved by someone, it's a terrific boost to your confidence. Knowing you are loved by God is the greatest confidence boost of all. So now, whenever doubt and dread besiege me, which they inevitably do, instead of collapsing like a wimp I whisper Zephaniah 3:17 to myself, and, having absorbed the power of these words, I stand tall. Try it – it really works! Halleluia!'

WENDY'S PRAYER

Father God, thank you for loving us and through your love strengthening us, so that we can go forward in the full confidence of knowing that we are your children, and that nothing can ever separate us from your love. Amen.

10

Jimmy Cricket

Jimmy is famed for his catch phrase, 'And there's more', but there really is more to Jimmy than meets the eye. With his special brand of family humour, Jimmy has enjoyed great success on stage, TV and radio, producing and writing many of his own shows.

His own family life was full of the qualities he incorporates in his act, such as natural good humour, kindness, warmth and a sense of fun. 'There are enough long faces in the world, and I don't plan to become one of them!' says Jimmy. He sees laughter as a very important release valve, and his job is to open it as wide as possible.

Jimmy was born into a large Irish family, with four brothers and one sister. His father was an undertaker by trade, so most people assumed that the family must have been miserable. But Jimmy remembers that it was completely the opposite. Their father had a wonderful sense of humour, and the house was always filled with laughter. Their house was also filled with the reality of God. Very much a God-fearing family, they attended church every Sunday. Jimmy says this is where his faith first took root.

Jimmy worked very hard in all aspects of show business before he literally became an overnight star, reaching the finals of ITV's *Search for a Star* and appearing in *A Night of 100 Stars* at the National Theatre. He had fine-tuned his act in the Northern Clubs, but one of his first jobs in the entertainment business was as a Butlin's Redcoat. For £6 a week he had to keep the children happy with games, entertain the adults, compere the contests and generally make sure that everyone had a good holiday. It was and still is the best training ground for any developing comic.

Three summer seasons at Butlin's passed before Jimmy swopped his red coat for a blue one, at Pontin's. It was to be not only a change of scene, but a change of life too, for it was here that he met his future wife, May.

'She was working as one half of an act called "The Tweedie Sisters", ' recalls Jimmy, 'and I couldn't take my eyes off her!' Two years later, in 1974, they were married. When they began a family, Jimmy developed his comic character in the Northern Clubs, his own ambitions now given added impetus by his desire to provide for May and the children.

'The wellies and stage gear came from experimenting,' Jimmy explains, 'and I picked up the hat in a jumble sale. The rolled-down wellies seemed a logical accessory for an illogical Irishman.'

For a comic to look funny, even before opening his mouth, is a real bonus, and Jimmy quickly found that he had this edge over his contemporaries. 'I looked daft, so audiences expected my act to be daft,' grins Jimmy, 'and I'm pleased to say that I have never disappointed them!'

Jimmy spends as much of his free time as possible with May and their four children. His favourite hobby is surrounding himself with happiness and contentment, and his strong faith is a very key part of that.

JIMMY'S FAVOURITE BIBLE VERSES

This is why I tell you not to be worried about the food and drink you need in order to stay alive, or about clothes for your body. After all, isn't life worth more than food? And isn't the body worth more than clothes? Look at the birds: they do not sow seeds, gather a harvest and put it in barns; yet your Father in heaven takes care of them! Aren't you worth much more than birds? Can any of you live a bit longer by worrying about it? ...

Instead, be concerned above everything else with the Kingdom of God and with what he requires of you, and he will provide you with all these other things. So do not worry about tomorrow; it will have enough worries of its own. There is no need to add to the troubles each day brings.

Matthew 6:25–34

'It's me, Jimmy! Come closer to the page!

'In our busy lives it's often the case that even when we manage to pick up our Bible and open it, we find ourselves skipping through it so quickly. Sometimes we are in danger of taking verses out of context, or allowing our mind to wander into thoughts about Sunday lunch in the middle of the church Bible reading. I know I can read something in the

Bible which I don't really understand, but then not take the time to look a little deeper. So why not, just for a moment, allow my show-biz catch phrase to help you take a closer look at this passage with me? Come closer!

'This particular passage says so much to me personally. I work in such a dodgy profession, for a start. The old show-business saying, "Don't ring us, we'll ring you" is quite true, and sometimes you never really know when the phone is going to ring. That goes for stars and chorus girls alike. One minute you are in great demand, and the next you wonder what the future holds. I never really know what the future holds, but I do know who holds the future!

'Looking at this passage, Jesus seems concerned with helping us to get our priorities right. He says we should put God first in our lives, instead of needlessly worrying about all the wrong things. It's certainly true that no amount of worrying ever solved a problem. It says in this verse that no one ever lived any longer by worrying! In fact, of course, it's quite the opposite. Worrying can lead to ulcers, stress and the many other physical symptoms of being unhappy. Jesus knows what he's talking about here.

'So how can we actually stop worrying, even when it seems that we are not going to be able to pay the bills this month? Well, because Jesus understands us so well, he knows how difficult it really is for us not to worry, and that's why the words 'Do not fear' appear 366 times in the Bible! God knows that I need to hear him say 'Don't worry!' every single day, with an extra 'Don't worry!' left over for leap years!

Having heard him say 'Don't worry', I then have to tell myself that he has good cause to tell me not to worry, and that I am worth a million times more than the sparrows that

God feeds. Many people in the entertainment business have a very low opinion of themselves in real life, and maybe that's why we need to hear your applause. We must try to grasp the fact that God really does love us, and that it's a love that can never be earned by you or me. He says that he actually cares about me and my problems, that he has everything safely in his hands, and that I must trust him again today.

'These words of Jesus are such a comfort to me. He knows and understands all the different pressures that I am under, and he smiles and says, "Hey, Jimmy, chill out – it's going to be all right!"'

JIMMY'S PRAYER

Heavenly Father, help me to relax when times are hard, and to know that there's a higher power guiding me. Give me the serenity to smile through the lean times, and give me the faith and confidence to know that if I do my best for you, everything else will be taken care of. And most of all, help me to use the talent you have given me to enrich people's lives with love and laughter. Through your Son, Jesus Christ. Amen.

11

Juliet Dawn

'The Juliet Dawn Foundation' has quickly become one of the most sought-after club acts in the country, winning the prestigious Mercury Award, 'Club Act of the Year 1997'. The threesome present a very lively and fast-moving show which features Juliet's stunning voice.

What her audiences would never imagine is that Juliet, and her husband Dave, are both committed Christians. The images most people have of religious people wearing opentoed sandals and carrying a heavy Bible around with them are shattered when you meet Juliet and Dave. Their enthusiasm for life and their enthusiasm for God show not just in their stage performance, but off stage too.

Juliet's mum and dad have been pastors of churches in both England and Spain. Six years spent in Spain exposed Juliet's parents to all the characters and casualties of life – from drug addicts to millionaires, from the homeless to people with very deep emotional problems. This, of course, meant that although Juliet was brought up in a Christian home, her parents were open-minded about whatever path she might decide to take in life.

After university Juliet was keen to forge a career as a television presenter, but with a very musical mother it was inevitable that Juliet would discover that the musical side of her was calling her into a different show business career.

Juliet says, 'After university, I needed an Equity union card to get into television, so I decided that the easiest way to do this was to get a summer season as a singer, not even knowing whether I would be any good. After several auditions I turned up for a job in Sheffield, where my future husband, Dave, was managing the cabaret venue. Dave listened intently to the only three songs I knew, and he was impressed, so I got the job! Sadly, nothing in show business lasts, and a few weeks later the venue closed.

'Dave decided to take me to Spain, knowing that there was a lot of cabaret work there. I stayed there with my parents, but little did we know what was going to happen next. Dave (who had been a Christian since he was 15 years old) re-committed his life to Christ, work was easy to come by, the weather was great, my parents were glad to have me at home and Dave and I fell in love!'

Juliet's parents were just as shocked as she was to see how well she sang, but they encouraged her talent as it progressed. After 18 months in Spain, Dave and Juliet became an established duo called 'Zocala' and were very successful. Eventually coming back to England, with equipment up to their eyeballs, they knew that they had a new fervour to tell others about their experiences of God.

The Juliet Dawn Foundation was formed in 1996 with the addition of another musician. Juliet and Dave agree that the hardest thing about being a Christian in show business is getting time to meet with other Christians. 'We also love to dispel people's preconceptions about what Christians are like. Christians are not boring, and our fast-moving, exciting show reflects what the Christian life is really all about for us.'

JULIET'S FAVOURITE BIBLE VERSE

You are my God;
teach me to do your will.
Be good to me, and guide me on a safe path.

Psalm 143:10

'This is King David's prayer, but so often in my quiet times I pray these words. I have no greater desire in my life than to continually be in the will of God and to live out his plans and purposes for my career, my family and friends, and for my future in general. However, the simplicity of the prayer does not reflect reality! Not knowing which path in life is God's will often leads me to personalize this passage as "Teach me to *know* your will."

'There are no rules in the entertainment business for becoming respected, being successful or discerning which opportunities to ignore and which to accept. Every time an offer presents itself, my husband and I so often discuss its possibilities from a human aspect, whereas our initial response should be to seek God. However, with our busy lifestyles, and the constant noise of different voices that surround us, it is sometimes very difficult to hear God's voice.

My Mum once told me wisely that if you feel an opportunity is worthy of attention, pray about it, then push the door gently and see if it opens. If it is the wrong thing, the door will close very quickly, or you will find it increasingly difficult to keep it open. Even when I've tried to push a door open because of my own selfish desires, I've found that God has not allowed me to push it open very far. From these valuable life lessons, I have learned the importance of trust and guidance in knowing and doing God's will.

'I have also learned that nobody gets it right all the time. So when I get it wrong, what then? David prayed that God would guide him forward on a safe path. This is important, because it means that we must trust God that, if what we are doing is not in his will, it will falter and begin to crumble. In my own life this scenario has happened so often – me doing my own thing, and God allowing difficulties and obstacles to be like huge "Danger" signs.

'Frequently, I have also wondered whether Satan was trying to make a mess of things. However, I know that although Satan will attack us as often as he can, he can never thwart God's plans for us, especially when we draw close to God.

'If in your own life you seek God's direction but feel that your life is on anything but a "safe path", then perhaps God is trying to show you that he has different plans for you. If this is the case, the most important thing for me and you is to do something about it.

'The most exciting thing is that even when we get it wrong, God is always ready to steer us back on course.'

JULIET'S PRAYER

My dearest Heavenly Father, I pray that my life will be full of your will and not mine. My own ways lack wisdom and are not alerted to pitfalls. My own ways are selfish but your ways are perfect, and are always the best for me, even when they don't seem that way. In everything I do today, help me to be Christlike, a shining light in dark places and a pearl of truth among ignorance and deceit. Teach me to be more sensitive to your voice of guidance, and to know when to act, as well as when not to. Most importantly, I pray that my life will not be tepid or half-hearted, nor a waste of the talent you have given me. I pray that I will use the gifts that you have entrusted to me to make a real difference for you. Amen.

12

Mike Doyle

'It's now medically proven that laughter helps to relieve depression, pain and anxiety. It stimulates yet relaxes, it gives every organ in the body a good work-out, and it's fun!' says Mike Doyle, himself a master of comedy. 'I really do think that laughter is God's medicine. Maybe I should be called a doctor instead of a comedian!'

Mike's unique blend of brilliant comedy matched with a truly fantastic singing voice has made him one of the country's top entertainers. But it was during one summer season engagement at Great Yarmouth that Mike got to the point when, as he puts it, he was laughing on the outside but crying on the inside.

It's Mike's job to make people laugh, of course, and if he comes off stage with the impression that he didn't get as many laughs as he could have done, he's disappointed. Comedy, as they say, is a very serious matter. It's even more serious if you don't feel like laughing yourself, and yet you have the job of getting several thousand audience members to roll about. On one occasion, just before going on stage for a pantomime matinee, Mike remembered that his five-year-old son Thomas was just about to go into another kind of theatre for a vital ear operation. Mike was hundreds of miles away and felt totally helpless, but the show had to go on.

Mike has been extremely successful in show business. He has had his own TV series and has starred in *Buddy* and *Grease* in London's West End. His breathtaking rendition of 'Nessun Dorma' during a Royal Variety Performance for Her Majesty the Queen stopped the show, and he repeated this in a Children's Royal Variety Show a year later. Mike is constantly in demand by all the major worldwide cruise lines and regularly stars in his own touring show, *Be My Love*, a tribute to Mario Lanza. Mike particularly looks forward to his regular pantomime seasons every Christmas.

However, he came to a point in his life where, although his career looked good, his personal life did not. He had had a Roman Catholic upbringing, but any thoughts about faith had been swallowed up by the all-enveloping world of show business. In any case, God seemed totally irrelevant to his life as a singer and comedian.

But now something had changed. He was not facing any particular crisis. Even though he spent a good deal of time away from home, his relationship with his wife, Jane, was good. Yet he felt desperately empty. Something was missing.

Being in Summer Season in Great Yarmouth meant that he was on the same bill as Cannon & Ball. Mike knew that Bobby was a Christian, but was very wary of him because both Bobby and Tommy had a terrible reputation in the business for being very aggressive, particularly towards the other acts, and most particularly towards other comedians.

It wasn't long, though, before Mike could recognize that a definite change had taken place in Bobby, and one day he took a deep breath and joined in a Bible study that Bobby was holding backstage in his dressing room before the evening performance. Mike was amazed at the incredible sense of God's presence in that place; he felt that God almost physically touched him. Mike actually wept that day because he had at last found what he had been looking for. God really was alive, and really did care about him and all his worries and problems. Mike got on his knees and surrendered his life to God.

The pastor who had led the Bible study promised to keep in touch, and encouraged Mike to start attending a lively church in Newport, near where Mike lived. Jane and their son Thomas went too. Eventually Jane made her own commitment to God.

Their faith has grown steadily over the years. Things have not been easy for them – it's difficult for both of them when Mike is away from home so much – but they know that God is now their source of strength.

Mike loves to point out how much laughter there is in the Bible. 'Some of the stories Jesus told would have been hilarious in his day and culture, ' says Mike. 'For example, imagine the man trying to get a speck out of his brother's eye while a huge log sticks out of his own! I also love Proverbs. There are some wonderful sayings in there like "A nagging wife is like a dripping tap"!

'Comedy demands a response, too. It's easier to remember what you've responded to in laughter. I think this is why

Jesus used funny stories. He wanted his audience to remember them because they all had something important to say about life.'

MIKE'S FAVOURITE BIBLE VERSES

> *There was once a man who had two sons. The younger one said to him, 'Father, give me my share of the property now' ... He went to a country far away, where he wasted his money in reckless living. He spent everything he had ... he was left without a thing ... He wished he could fill himself with the bean pods the pigs ate, but no one gave him anything to eat. At last he came to his senses and said ... 'I will get up and go to my father and say, "Father, I have sinned against God and against you. I am no longer fit to be called your son"' ... So he got up and started back to his father.*
>
> *He was still a long way from home when his father saw him ... and he ran, threw his arms round his son, and kissed him.*
>
> **Luke 15:11–32**

'I just love this story. Sometimes it goes round and round in my head and I consider every aspect of it. How the Father loved his son enough to let him go in the first place, and how easy it is to spend money!

'It makes me think of my own son, Thomas. When he's having a bad day and doesn't do what I say, he gets cross, throws a tantrum and then runs up to his bedroom and slams the door. How often I have done that to Father God when he doesn't give me what I want!

'I keep listening carefully, because it's normally about half an hour later that Thomas will come slowly down the stairs, sidle quietly into our front room and whisper "Sorry, Daddy" in my ear.

'So, what do I do? Shout and scream at him to make him feel really bad? Make him do the washing up for a week? Or tell him to do 20 press-ups? No, of course not! His word of apology makes my father's heart jump, and almost makes we want to cry because I know he means it, and I love him so much. Hugs all round, and everything is fine between us again.

'It's just like that with my heavenly Daddy too. I know I will fall, I know I'll get cross with God, I even know that I am capable of running away from him. But I also know that he will be there, watching and waiting for me to return, my tail between my legs, ready to say a very humble "Sorry."

'Does he holler at me and send huge punishments down on me? No, though it's possible that my sin may have some other effect. He wraps his arms around me and welcomes me back home. Some mistakes I seem to make over and over again, and yet I know he's always ready to forgive.'

MIKE'S PRAYER

Dear Father, help me never to forget that, no matter how many times I get it wrong, you are always there to hear my words of apology and welcome me back into your arms. Help me to forgive others in the same way too. Amen.

13

Eternal

For the new all-girl singing group 'Eternal', the 1994 Children's Royal Variety Performance was their most important show to date. It was watched by HRH Princess Margaret and several million television viewers. Since those early days, 'Eternal' have stormed the music charts in every possible way. With numerous consecutive hit singles in the UK, the USA, Australia and Japan, they are one of the most successful girl bands ever. Amazingly, they have reached the top 15 with every single they have released to date.

It's hard work, though, and while the girls enjoy some of the glamour that their popularity affords, there are many sacrifices to be made too, particularly in the area of family, friends and social life. There just isn't time to make any real friendships. They believe that if they work hard for a few years now in order to establish themselves, hopefully they will later be able to slow down a little and think about other things than just show business.

The old saying that 'two's company, three's a crowd' is certainly not true in the case of 'Eternal'. Easther and Vernie Bennett are sisters, and Kelle was with them since the band was formed, and they all get on well together, even when forced to spend a lot of their time together.

All of them are committed Christians, and they still make time to pray backstage before each performance. They feel it's important to say 'Thank you' for yet another opportunity to use the gifts that God has given them. In fact, for Easther and Vernie their earliest experience of singing was in church, where their mother was a pastor.

They have never hidden their Christianity, and have realized that they have many opportunities to be open about their spirituality in front of the world's media. Their albums and singles also often contain lyrics which unmistakably express the girls' Christian faith. It's also important for them to show that a belief in God doesn't mean that you have to be boring – in fact, quite the opposite.

They believe that their success is partly due to their unwillingness to sell their records by using sexy images. Deliberately side-stepping the temptation to be a sexually based group, they feel that an image that shows them being more in control, particularly through their complicated dance routines, is more attractive to their audience.

The girls don't want to be another 'flash in the pan' band either, so they have set their minds on creating a solid working base that will sustain them for many years to come. They are obviously keen to live up to their name, 'Eternal'. Their *Greatest Hits* album was released in 1997, and if the past few years are anything to go by, there are many more albums just around the corner.

EASTHER'S FAVOURITE BIBLE VERSE

We know that in all things God works for good with those who love him, those whom he has called according to his purpose.

Romans 8:28

Easther says, 'This is the verse that really seems to fill up my heart at the moment. I believe that God makes "all things work for good" because I feel that if it wasn't for the Lord I wouldn't be in such a successful group as "Eternal". And I feel that if I keep on believing in him and letting the Lord choose my path for good or for bad, it will always be the right one, for there's a reason for everything in life.'

Easther also realizes that this is one of the most misunderstood verses in the Bible. Why? Because some people take it to mean that when we become Christians nothing bad will ever happen to us. This, of course, is not true.

'We still live in a corrupt world. We only have to look at today's newspapers to see how prevalent evil is in our society,' Easther explains. 'However, God is bigger than all that, and shows us the way of repentance and that he really is the Almighty.'

The verse talks about 'all things' too. So often we desperately want to see God at work in isolated incidents, but he is concerned with changing every circumstance into our long-range good. He can see things from a distance much more easily than we can. Although it may seem at times that God isn't sorting it out as you would like him to, he really does know best.

What's really great is that this verse is one of God's personal promises. It's not just for anybody, though. It's only for those who love him and are part of his special family. As Easther says, 'I know that I must trust him and let him choose the path for my life, in the good times and the bad. I understand that it will always be the right path, because God will always be able to take all that life throws at me and eventually use it for good.'

EASTHER'S PRAYER

'When I was young, I used to recite this prayer. It was a way of saying that I was happy to trust God in everything and to place my life totally in his hands.'

When I lay me down to sleep
I pray, dear Lord, my soul to keep.
If I should die before I wake
I pray, dear Lord, my soul to take. Amen.

14

Beth Ellis

Born and raised in Singapore, Beth Ellis trained at RADA and made her debut professional appearance at Belfast's Arts Theatre. This first job led to a ten-year stay in Northern Ireland. While there she formed and ran Northern Ireland's first repertory company. She also worked as a presenter and interviewer on Ulster Television's first weekly women's programme, *Women Only*, and scripted and compered fashion shows. In addition she ran a model school and agency, a weekend drama school for young people and Ulster's first and only Charm School!

Her West End stage appearances have been numerous, including *Alibi for a Judge* with Andrew Cruickshank, and the world's longest-running play, *The Mousetrap*. She has starred in many touring shows and repertory seasons and has appeared on television in *Crossroads*, *Brookside*, *Z Cars* and *Eastenders*.

Beth married the actor Jimmy Ellis in 1956. He was well known as Bert Lynch, the police receptionist in the popular TV police series *Z Cars*. Sadly, with all the different pressures on their careers, the marriage was not to last, and they separated in 1964. For Beth, 20 years of touring plays and repertory followed, juggling work with the needs of their children.

One day an event occurred which was to change her life for ever. Beth takes up the story. 'I was sitting watching the six o'clock news. The phone rang. It was my son's current girlfriend. "Hello, Beth. Is Adam there? We'd arranged to go to the Proms tonight, but the boys in the house say he hasn't been home. I was wondering if he had stayed with you."

'It was a Friday in August 1988. Adam was my middle son, aged 28. Scina had left him fishing at the canal near Sainsbury's at around 9 p.m. the night before, and no one had seen him since. Suddenly I heard the TV announcer say, "West London police are trying to identify the body of a young man found stabbed on the towpath of the Grand Union Canal, apparently while fishing."

'I didn't realize it then, but that news was going to change my life. Adam was a committed Christian, though neither my younger son nor my daughter nor I had any real belief. However, we naturally turned to Adam's friends and the curate at his church, who helped us to organize the funeral. Once this was over I suggested that out of courtesy we must visit the church where Adam had worshipped.

'Arriving at the service, I was overwhelmed by the sense of commitment to a Lord I did not know. Musicians played songs with beautiful words like "Be still – for the power of the Lord is moving in this place." I could feel God's presence there, and I wept.

'Seven years later, Adam's brother Hugo married Rachel, one of those young musicians. My daughter Amanda has also committed her life to Jesus. I'm reminded of Jesus's words: "a grain of wheat remains no more than a single grain unless it is dropped into the ground and dies. If it does die, then it produces many grains"' (John 12:24).

Beth is today as busy as she has always been, and keen to serve God in any way that he should wish. She has a particular sympathy for those who are poorer than herself, and has spent many years working with the international relief group YWAM.

Joining the Christians in Entertainment Bible studies in the West End during her spell in *The Mousetrap*, Beth learned that poverty is not always physical. Seeing the spiritual poverty that is so evident in her own profession, Beth spent a year with the CIE team travelling around the country to encourage and support those working in the isolation that show business often creates.

Beth looks back over a career that has been so special, in so many different ways. But she looks forward too, knowing that God always has the next part of his plan for her life just 'waiting in the wings'.

BETH'S FAVOURITE BIBLE VERSE

I am telling you the truth: a grain of wheat remains no more than a single grain unless it is dropped into the ground and dies. If it does die, then it produces many grains.

John 12:24

'This was such a difficult choice to make. I keep finding new verses that seem to be so relevant at the time of reading. They just jump off the page and speak to me about some situation that I may be wrestling with on that precise day, and I have to add them to my list of favourite verses.

'For example, I first began to understand how precious I am to God, how very much I am loved by him, when I read "You did not choose me; I chose you and appointed you to go and bear much fruit, the kind of fruit that endures" [John 15:16]. This blew my mind! It was such an awesome idea – wow! It was also such a responsibility, but what a privilege too!

'When I chose to take a sabbatical after 40 years of show biz, I wanted to try to learn how to be a "star" in God's kingdom. So, I enrolled on a twelve-week course with Youth With a Mission called a Discipleship Training School. As a new Christian I found the course a very challenging time. I was surrounded by about 70 mature Christians from many different social and cultural backgrounds. I felt such a novice! Up on the wall of our main classroom was a big sign bearing a promise that I clung to: "And so I am sure that God, who began this good work in you, will carry it on until it is finished on the Day of Christ Jesus" [Philippians 1:6]. Nine years into this new adventure, every time I stumble, I suddenly see that big sign on the classroom wall, and I'm encouraged to go on.

'However, I've been asked for my favourite verse of all, and I think this has to be the verse about the seed dying, from John's Gospel.

'Let me explain this. When my first-born son, Adam, was murdered, the knife that pierced his heart also killed a part of me as well. Adam was a committed Christian, but neither I nor his sister Amanda nor his younger brother Hugo had any faith at all. However, through this traumatic time and in our own vulnerability, all of us discovered at first hand the love and comfort that was so freely available from God through his family in our local church. We had made the wonderful discovery that he was creating new lives in all of us.

'Amanda wrote at the time of Adam's death: "And through His love, His joy, the sadness flew away, and I emerged a new creation."

'I just go on telling people that these wonderful promises from the Bible are true. Go ahead and claim them for yourself!'

BETH'S PRAYER

Lord, make me an instrument of your peace.
Where there is hatred, let me sow love.
Where there is injury, let me pardon.
Where there is doubt, let me bring faith.
Where there is despair, let me bring hope.
Where there is darkness, let me be light.
Where there is sadness, let me bring joy. Amen.

15

Steve Fortune

Steve's first job in show business was as a dancer in a cabaret show which toured Europe and the Middle East. Upon his return to England Steve worked in summer season and pantomime before getting his first West End show, *Underneath the Arches*, in which he understudied the role of Chesney Allen. Steve says, 'It was on this show that I met my wife Tracy, who was working as an usherette at the time. It was also on this show that I first met Chris and Trinity from Christians in Entertainment, but it was to be a few years before we met again.'

After *Underneath the Arches* Steve worked around the country in various repertory theatres in shows such as *Annie*, *Sweet Charity*, *The Music Man* and *The Pirates of Penzance*. He also worked at the Chichester Festival Theatre in *Annie Get Your Gun*, which subsequently transferred to the Aldwych in London for a limited run. In 1990 he was back in the West

End again in the hit musical *Chess*. Steve's TV work has included *Only Fools and Horses*, *Birds of a Feather*, *Nelson's Column*, *Casualty*, *Back Up* and *The Bill*. 'I've also appeared in a number of commercials, advertising everything from Woodstain to Bananas!' laughs Steve.

Tracy has also continued in the business. After working in the wardrobe department in a number of West End theatre shows, Tracy moved to BBC Television, and has enjoyed working on *Eastenders*, where she has been since 1993.

'It was the birth of our son which brought Tracy and I into the Church and into our relationship with Christ.' Having been baptized in the Church of England, Steve and Tracy approached the vicar of their local church to arrange for their son Jack to be baptized. The vicar agreed but pointed out that he felt strongly that baptism is a sacrament and that by having their son baptized they were making a commitment to God which they should continue to honour.

'He asked us to "give church a chance", to attend for a time and see how we liked it, ' remarks Steve. 'On reflection, it would have been easy to agree, have the baptism and never return again, but that was not God's plan for us.'

Honouring their promise, Steve and Tracy began to attend the church, and discovered a community of people with whom they shared common ground. 'We made friends, and my gifts as an actor were useful for reading and for other events that happened in the life of the church, and our involvement became greater and greater. On 28 January 1996 Tracy and I were both confirmed. This meant that we acknowledged that Jesus was now Lord of our lives.'

It is interesting to note that in the same year Steve was cast in the revival of Andrew Lloyd Webber's and Tim Rice's production of *Jesus Christ Superstar*, which resurrected London's Lyceum Theatre after a gap of 25 years.

How did Steve feel about being in such a show? 'Well, as a Christian it was an opportunity through the medium of theatre to tell the story of the passion. Although previous productions of the show had possibly trivialized the story, the director of this new production, Gale Edwards, wanted it to be more realistic and moving. The response from people who have seen the show has confirmed that it is very thought provoking, and indeed has caused a number of people to re-examine their own feelings.

'There have been criticisms of the show, and certain liberties have been taken with the Gospel for dramatic reasons. For example, many of the actions associated with women have been grouped together and attributed to Mary Magdalene. But this is theatrical licence, and if at the end of the show people go away thinking about the life of Christ and his awful death on the cross, then surely the show is "shining as a light to the world", and that can't be a bad thing.

'Whilst in the West End I have discovered Christians in Entertainment anew, and their example prompted me to suggest to other Christians in the show that we should get together regularly for Bible study and prayer, and that is what we did. I think it's very appropriate to have a Bible study on *Jesus Christ Superstar*!'

STEVE'S FAVOURITE BIBLE VERSES

I may be able to speak the languages of men and even of angels, but if I have no love, my speech is no more than a

noisy gong or a clanging bell. I may have the gift of inspired
preaching; I may have all knowledge and understand all
secrets; I may have all the faith needed to move mountains –
but if I have no love, I am nothing.

1 Corinthians 13:1–2

'I have never really been one for favourites. I can't think of
my favourite film or book, and as I am not a football fan, I
don't have a favourite team. So when I was asked for my
contribution to this book, I really couldn't think of one verse
which I would prefer above any other.

'Actually, it makes me rather glad to think that God does-
n't have any favourites either. Imagine if he did. I don't think
most of us would make the grade. So I'm so thankful that his
love for me doesn't depend on who I am, whether I'm good
at my job, whether I'm married, where I was born, what
colour my skin is or how often I go to church!

'As I looked through my Bible, however, I remembered all
those books which have been the greatest encouragement for
me since I became a Christian. Ecclesiastes – difficult to pro-
nounce, but full of advice on how to live a godly life; Isaiah,
with its wonderful prophecies; and, of course, the Gospels,
for their accounts of Jesus's life and teaching, and his final
sacrifice made for all mankind.

'Finding that some of the most thought-provoking and
inspirational teachings in the Bible come from St Paul's letters, it was here that I finally decided upon my favourite
verse. Without love everything else is a waste of time, he
says. Jesus said that the greatest commandment was to love
the Lord your God with all your soul, your mind and your
strength, as well as loving your neighbour as yourself.

'Here in his letter to the new Christian church in Corinth, Paul challenges their priority list. How often we are tempted to try to look good in front of other Christians, using the public gifts. How often do we eagerly seek an opportunity to be heard in church, rather than to make the tea afterwards?

'Throughout the whole of chapter 13, Paul says again and again that no matter how clever or gifted we may be, without love we have nothing.

'"Oh, that's all easier said than done," I hear you say. "How on earth am I supposed to love my next-door neighbour when his music blasts out the window at three o'clock in the morning? How can I love the person who just lied to me?" This is probably where we need God's help the most. Loving the unlovable is something that God does all the time, and we must learn to do the same.

'We are called by God to live as he would have us live, and the doorway by which we enter that life is love.

A PRAYER FOR LOVE

Grant, O Lord, that your unimaginable Love
May find in me some love to meet it.
Let me love the Love that ever loves me.
Let my soul's delight be to love you
And what you love,
And whom you love,
Now and always, life without end.
Through your Son, Jesus Christ.
Amen.

16

Peter Goodwright

In his busy career, Peter Goodwright has tackled most aspects of show business. For nearly 40 years his work in broadcasting has been prolific, with cabaret, after-dinner speaking, stage performances and cruising taking him all over the world.

Peter has had many of his own series on radio and television, and has been a guest on almost every variety show. He has appeared at the country's most prestigious venues, like the Albert Hall and the London Palladium. With all that experience behind him, he is amused to be frequently described as a 'veteran' performer!

Peter met his wife, Norma, when she was working with the George Mitchell Black and White Minstrel Company. They actually met on a Ken Dodd show. Their wedding was an idyllic ceremony in a pretty village church. They were given the red-carpet treatment by crowds of well-wishers, and press photographers captured the special day of a well-known celebrity of the time.

This public image of their life together – popular acclaim and monetary success – continued for several years, but underneath, they were both aware of a missing piece in the apparently successful jigsaw of their life. Both Peter and Norma saw the need for a more fulfilling meaning to their rather shallow and worldly existence. As children they had both gone to church and Sunday school but, like so many people, they had drifted away from church as they had grown into the worldly niche they had made for themselves.

Habit took them to church at Christmas and Easter, but it was only when their son Tim was to be baptized in 1970 that they were once more drawn into the family of the Church. They thank God that he placed them in an area where there was a very alive and welcoming Anglican church.

In arranging the christening, the vicar was very kind and co-operative, and so, more out of politeness than worship, they attended his church for the next few Sundays. Peter and Norma just thought it was a lucky 'coincidence' that their rare church visits coincided with visiting speakers like David Watson, a great evangelist who had the gift of relating the gospel message to our culture today. Now they can see that they were there as part of God's plan for their future. Peter and Norma no longer believe in 'coincidences', but rather in 'God-incidences'!

David Watson talked about the good news of Jesus Christ, and explained that God wasn't just 'somebody up there', powerful and remote, but rather, he was a personal God who knew each and every one of us and who cared about the way we lived our lives.

That was the missing piece in Peter and Norma's apparently successful jigsaw. Norma was the first to accept this good news and to commit her life to Christ, but it took only a few weeks for Peter to do the same.

PETER AND NORMA'S FAVOURITE BIBLE VERSES

Peter's: I have the strength to face all conditions by the power that Christ gives me.

Philippians 4:13

Norma's: And I will be with you always, to the end of the age.

Matthew 28:20

'Having Jesus in our lives has now put our priorities into perspective and has given us a firm faith and confidence to face whatever the future holds. We smile when people say, "Oh, it's all right for you, because being a Christian means you don't have any worries or problems!"

'*Wrong*! We have found that trusting in Jesus doesn't mean that you are given a magic wand. In fact, we now believe that if anyone is finding the Christian life easy, then they're not doing it right!

'Following the Lord's teachings can be very hard indeed – it's impossible without his help. We rejoice in the comforting knowledge that the power of the Holy Spirit and the all-embracing love of the Father enfolds us at all times.

'This is why these verses mean so much to us. What a wonderful God we worship. Praise be!'

PETER AND NORMA'S PRAYER

Heavenly Father, we thank you for your kindness and loving care for us at all times and in all places.

We thank you for our blessed Lord Jesus, whose teachings and example we strive to follow.

We thank you for the strength and power you give us through your Holy Spirit, and for the opportunities you give us to share our faith.

We love you more than we can say, and we know that it is much less than you love us. Amen.

17

Philip Griffiths

Philip Griffiths must be one of the longest serving members of London's West End theatre. He has been in a variety of productions since 1978, and not only is he currently appearing in Andrew Lloyd Webber's *Phantom of the Opera* but he has been on that production for the past seven years.

Having toured with most of the UK's leading opera companies, doing the same show night after night is something Philip has got quite used to. Instead of being bored, however, he finds that having a different audience every night brings some measure of freshness to each performance. Philip, who lives with his wife Susan and their daughters Anna and Sîan near Brighton, also enjoys the moderate stability that the West End can sometimes bring. His many other West End musicals include *Chess*, *Biograph Girl* and *Anything Goes*, but it was during the eight-year run of *Evita* that Philip helped to make history.

Evita was Tim Rice's and Andrew Lloyd Webber's latest musical, and the country was buzzing with excitement, waiting to see what was said to be a landmark musical phenomenon. Indeed it was. The huge metal set, the lit floor, the brilliant lyrics and score, but above all the subject matter caught the audience's imagination. Gone were the dancing girls of the traditional musical. Here was the story of one woman's phenomenal rise to power, and her tragic death.

Philip remembers that the show started with a funeral and finished with a funeral, and this didn't help the morale of the cast. In fact some of them became depressed, and, after one member of the cast had committed suicide, it was even said that there was a curse on the theatre.

During this time two new members joined the cast, and they happened to be Christians. They both felt that the spiritual atmosphere at the theatre was very heavy, and they both prayed individually for support and fellowship. Imagine their surprise when one day they discovered each other's faith because a book by Billy Graham had been left on a dressing-room table. Immediately they knew their prayers had been answered, and they started to meet together each week in their dressing room.

Theatres are small communities where gossip is often rife, and it didn't take long for the rest of the theatre, and eventually the entire West End, to hear about this strange Christian meeting going on backstage at the Prince Edward Theatre.

Despite having been brought up in a Christian home, Philip found that his faith had recently become a little stale. He found it too easy to leave God in church every Sunday. He had heard about the new weekly meeting, but had decided to stay away. Describing himself as a doubting Thomas, he had imagined that a backstage Bible study was probably the most boring thing around. When he heard other members of the cast talking enthusiastically about the time they had spent together, he decided to give it a try. When he joined in the following week, Philip was delighted. It was not as he had imagined – this was something different. It was interesting, personal and very exciting. Here was an opportunity to see the relevance of God right there in his place of work.

The small group that met each week soon expanded, at one stage numbering 13. Philip found the Bible study, the teaching and especially the prayer a great source of help, inspiration and encouragement. By now many different people from many West End theatres were cramming into the tiny backstage room. Just a year later, in 1982, Philip became one of the founder members of the newly formed 'Christians in Entertainment' charity.

Many of the cast on *Evita* commented on the fact that the atmosphere at the theatre had changed, and that the show seemed much easier to work on. In the end, *Evita* ran for nearly eight years, and Philip likes to think that God's special involvement may have had something to do with the success it enjoyed.

In 1995 many Christians appearing in different shows all over the West End were brought together for a special one-off performance to celebrate the presence of God in the London theatres over the past 10 years. *West-End Praise* was filmed by the BBC and was transmitted as a special programme in their *Songs of Praise* series. Philip was one of the people featured in that programme.

Bible studies and prayer groups still meet backstage each week, and Christians in Entertainment is still active in the

West End, but Philip is proud to have been one of the first who saw God's light and love shine into the very closed world of the London theatre.

PHILIP'S FAVOURITE BIBLE VERSE

For the Lord watches over the righteous and listens to their prayers.

1 Peter 3:12

'Have you ever felt that your prayers are just hitting the ceiling? So have I. Over the past two years Susan and I have struggled with a very difficult medical condition that one of our daughters has had to endure. Sometimes the symptoms have been extremely worrying, but because the doctors could not give a full diagnosis or guarantee a successful treatment, we were often left in total darkness. We didn't know what the outcome of all this suffering would be, and it's always the unknown which is the most frightening thing. Our prayers, calling out to God to heal our daughter, seemed to be empty. Yet we knew he was there, and we had to learn, using all our energy, to trust him.

'I remember that in one of the *Evita* Bible studies someone said that God is never disillusioned with us, because he never has any illusions about us in the first place! In other words, God knows what we are capable of, and he understands how hard it is for us to trust him sometimes. The most difficult times are when he seems to be silent.

'God also knows that we forget so easily, so he repeats things to us again and again. That is why this verse is important to me. It's reminding me that even when it doesn't seem like it, God is watching over us, and he does hear our prayers. It's a promise that he will never break. Hang on to it!'

PHILIP'S PRAYER

What a friend we have in Jesus,
All our sins and grief to bear.
What a privilege to carry
Everything to God in Prayer.
Oh what peace we often forfeit,
Oh what needless pain we bear,
All because we do not carry
everything to God in Prayer.

18

George Hamilton IV

1996 marked George Hamilton IV's fortieth year in the music industry, and he's loved every minute of it. He is the USA's best-loved Country singer, and his records have sold in their millions. He has toured the world in musicals, and he became an international pop star with hits like 'Abilene' and 'Before this Day Ends'.

George is included on the 'Sidewalk to the Stars' at the Country Music Hall of Fame, and *Billboard* magazine gave him the title of 'International Ambassador of Country Music'. Indeed, George Hamilton IV has taken his own special brand of Country music to many countries around the world, and he spends much of each year on tour, then returning to his home in Franklin, Tennessee.

However, it is George's love of Country Gospel Music that is closest to his heart, supported by a deep and sincere Christian faith. George likes nothing more than to sing about his love of Jesus, and many of his secular albums have tracks which are obviously Gospel based. He spends several months of the year touring the UK with his familiar festive concerts based around Easter, Christmas and, of course, Thanksgiving.

His proudest moments have seen him touring with the best-known Christian evangelist in the world, Billy Graham. On his first date with Billy, it was noted that George won many hearts through his simple, direct and heart-warming songs. It was obvious that what George was singing was really coming from his heart, and coming from God's heart too.

GEORGE'S FAVOURITE BIBLE VERSE

> *So then ... because of God's great mercy to us I appeal to you: Offer yourselves as a living sacrifice to God, dedicated to his service and pleasing to him. This is the true worship that you should offer.*

Romans 12:1

'"Worshipping God" does not just mean going to church on a Sunday. We need to worship God all the time, in every place, and in any circumstance. Why? Because when we focus on God, it reminds us who the real boss-man is!

'The problem is that sometimes we think we are the boss. In my business, faced with an artiste's insecurity, we often find it easy to hide behind our egos. I work in an industry that is so often absorbed with "self". The star of the show often carries a very heavy responsibility to make the show work. If the box office takings are low, you take it very personally, and you wonder if the producer will hire you the next time. The rest of the cast look to you as the leader of the company, so exposing your own insecurities can have the effect of bringing them low too.

'It's true that performers do need confidence to face an audience, though. We have to believe that we really are the best actor, musician, whatever, but if we pretend that our gifts and abilities are of our own making, that's where we start to come unstuck. No, the credit for our talents must go to God, and this verse helps me to remember that I must continually offer my talents back to the One who gave them to me in the first place.

'When I speak, think, perform, I try and imagine whether my heavenly Father would be pleased with the way I did it. Every performance I do I offer as a living sacrifice to him. That doesn't mean I always sing Gospel songs or talk only about Jesus. I just try and do my best in whatever situation I am in, because I want to please him, in each day that he gives me.'

A MUSICIAN'S PRAYER

Dear Father, make us your instruments – like musical instruments that stay in tune with you! On us, in us and through us, play your music – your way! Amen!

19

Derek Jefferson

He was known as the hard man of football. During the late sixties and the seventies the central defender of Ipswich Town was even dubbed 'Chopper' by team-mates and fans alike. The superb skills of this no-nonsense action man of soccer were coveted and feared by many opposition players.

He took this tough-guy image with him to Wolverhampton Wanderers in 1972, but off the pitch his personal life was falling apart. After a brief spell playing in the States, he returned to the UK, but his wife and two children had already left him.

This was a turning-point for Derek. 'If there really is a God,' he thought, 'I need him right now!' Derek recalls, 'I came back from the States to take up the job of a Player/Manager at Yeovil Town. But when I rang the chairman before going down there, he said that he had given the job to someone else! I was totally devastated, and I didn't think I could be involved in football ever again.

'So I did what gave me comfort on occasions like this. I drank too much and drove my car too fast. Ending up in Worcester Hospital with concussion, I heard that my car was a total write-off and that it was amazing that I was still alive. After three days, I returned to an empty house. I cried out to God, but nothing happened.

'Six weeks later I was visiting my parents in Middlesbrough, when my Mum asked me to come to church on the Sunday evening. Amazingly enough, I accepted. Once there, I heard a young man talking about Jesus – about his sacrifice on the cross, and how everything could be forgiven if we would let him do things his way and not our way.

'I broke down and cried, and asked God to forgive me. I will never forget the sense of peace I had at that moment.'

Now, Derek loves nothing better than passing on some of his soccer skills and techniques to others. He holds regular residential camps with tailor-made coaching and sports activities for children, teenagers and adults. These are sometimes church based, and he uses his skills to show that God is interested in sport, that the Bible often talks about life as winning a race, and that with God beside us, we will always be on the winning side.

DEREK'S FAVOURITE BIBLE VERSE

I have come in order that you might have life – life in all its fullness.

John 10:10

'I thought that as a professional footballer, I had life. I travelled the world, stayed in the best hotels, and enjoyed the adulation of the crowds. At that time, in my pre-Christian days, that was real life for me. What else did I need? Getting transferred for more and more money, buying bigger and better houses, getting faster and more expensive cars. What more could I want? I even went to the USA and played against Pelé. I was in great demand, I felt important, and I was earning a lot of money.

'Life like this can be great fun, of course. The problem is that it hardly ever lasts, and when you rely solely on all the material things of life to keep you happy and fulfilled, you come down to earth with a big bump when it stops. The desire for material things can often dazzle us, and this can cause us to be blind to the fact that we have spiritual needs too.

'My career suddenly seemed to end at the same time as my marriage, and a near-fatal car crash brought me to my senses. I believe that God had his hand on me at that time, and when I came out of hospital I knew there had to be more to life. I still had all the material possessions I needed, but I was feeling empty and unfulfilled.

'The day I found myself in church, I heard a man talking about Jesus as if he was real. I had memories of Bible stories about Jesus, but surely, I thought, they were all just fairy tales. And yet this man talked as if he knew Jesus personally. I suddenly knew what was missing in my life. I realized that in all my attempts to reach the top of the ladder of success, I had actually been climbing the wrong ladder. Accepting Jesus Christ into my life was the best thing I ever did. He filled the aching gap that I felt inside of me, and I felt totally new.

'God is not someone boring sitting on a big throne in heaven. He is not trying to bog us down with rules and regulations which take all the fun out of living. Rather, he is an amazing God who is full of life, vitality and fun. He wants you and me to be fulfilled. Not just with the things that look very attractive at first but don't really last, but with the exciting and special plan that he has for each one of us.'

DEREK'S PRAYER

Father, you made me aware that I was pleasing myself and not pleasing you. Now, as I trust and rely on you each day, I can see what you mean about having a really abundant life. I understand that we live in a material world which often ignores you. I know that you don't want to take those things away from us, but rather, you want us to recognize what is more important. Help me to recognize this today. Amen.

20

Paul Jones and Fiona Hendley

Paul and Fiona must be the busiest married couple in show business! Paul, well known as the lead singer of the sixties group 'Manfred Mann', is remembered for such hits as 'Do Wah Diddy' and 'Pretty Flamingo'. His numerous television appearances include starring as 'Uncle Jack' for the BBC, while millions listen to his programmes on Radio 2 and Jazz FM.

Paul's theatre career ranges from the Royal National Theatre and the Royal Shakespeare Company to the West End and Broadway. He has several Gold Discs, stretching from the days of Manfred Mann to the original album of *Evita* and his own group The Blues Band, which has recorded numerous albums.

Fiona, an accomplished actress and singer, has worked extensively in all areas of the business, from her acclaimed television series *Widows* to leading roles at the Royal National Theatre and the Royal Shakespeare Company. Fiona is often seen starring in the West End in a whole range of musicals, dramas and comedies.

It was while working together at the Royal National Theatre that Paul and Fiona first met. Paul had been invited to watch the theatre's original production of *Guys and Dolls* and was immediately struck by this actress dancing on stage. He just couldn't take his eyes off her! Paul was soon to be cast as the fiery Macheath in the National Theatre's new production of *The Beggars' Opera*. He was delighted to find that this same girl was also in the cast.

Fiona remembers that her first conversation with Paul was extremely embarrassing. She thought he had been part of the band 'Herman's Hermits'! Paul managed to forgive her mistake, and they were soon seeing each other off-stage as much as on. They had played lovers in their opposite roles in *The Beggars' Opera*, and they were now cast as lovers in *Guys and Dolls* too.

Without realizing it, they were both on a search for spiritual things. Paul, a confirmed atheist, was so dogmatic that he had been hired to confront Cliff Richard's faith on a television debate. However, his hobby of looking at paintings led him to eventually acknowledge that there was another dimension to life – a spiritual one. All his rational, logical and intellectual pretences crumbled when he realized that he was dealing with something that actually bypassed all of that.

Fiona had been searching for a spiritual meaning to life for some while. Having been drawn in by the Moonies cult at one stage, she was wary of making any moves towards religion, and yet she was desperate to discover the truth. One day, finishing a broadcast for the BBC earlier than expected,

Fiona decided to pop into the church next door to Broadcasting House. Enjoying the peaceful atmosphere, she opened a Bible, and was excited to read a passage that talked about how much God loved people.

In her quest to discover more, Fiona started attending church, with Paul joining her. The opportunity to attend some Bible studies, giving them a chance to ask some serious questions about Christian beliefs, was a landmark in their journey. Not long afterwards they were amazed to get a telephone call from the very person whom Paul had argued against in that television debate.

Cliff Richard was inviting them to come and hear an evangelist called Luís Palau. They accepted the invitation, and, having heard the evangelist speak so clearly about how they were feeling, they could only agree that God was speaking directly and personally to them. God was answering their plea to know whether he really existed and really cared about them. They found out that he not only cared about them but loved them. They received God's love and asked him to be Lord of their lives. They have never regretted it.

PAUL AND FIONA'S FAVOURITE BIBLE VERSES

Whoever goes to the Lord for safety,
whoever remains under the protection of the Almighty,
can say to him, 'You are my defender and protector.
You are my God; in you I trust.'

Psalm 91:1–2

'There's a place we can be with the Lord where we are safe – Psalm 91 says so. Isn't that wonderful?

'While we are on this earth, we are in a spiritual battle. Ephesians says, "we are not fighting against human beings but against the wicked spiritual forces in the heavenly world" (Ephesians 6:12). The devil is prowling around trying to destroy and steal, speaking negative words into people's minds and generally trying to crush them. God loves us so much, though, that he has given us a mighty suit of armour to wear, to protect us in our everyday lives – even through the toughest of storms.

'One of the most powerful weapons we have is God's mighty two-edged sword, which is his Word, the Bible. Jesus used God's Word in this way when he was fasting in the desert, and the devil came to taunt and tempt him. Jesus constantly said, "It is written …" and then spoke a scripture appropriate to the temptation. The devil finally gave up and ran away. Elsewhere in the Bible, James says, "Resist the Devil, and he will run away from you" (James 4:7).

'We have found that Psalm 91 gives us the most comforting and glorious strength. We don't always know what our day is going to bring, so before we do anything else, we spend some time with our Heavenly Father, telling him about our worries, letting him know that we place our day before him, and putting on our spiritual armour: salvation, right standing with God, his truth, peace, faith and his Word (see Ephesians 6:11–17). Then we pray Psalm 91, putting ourselves into its words: "*We* who go to the Lord for safety …" It really is a fantastic way to start the day!

'This Psalm promises real protection: it is possible to live free from fear in a dangerous and unpredictable world. But, as verse one says, this protection is for those who *go* to the Lord, for those who *abide* with God, who live in continual union with him, keeping his Word, obeying his voice. If we are in that secret place with God, we can live without dread of what the devil will do. So even when life gets like a hurricane, God promises to deliver us. Just read the final two verses. This is God's reply back to us: "When they call to me, I will answer them; when they are in trouble, I will be with them. I will rescue them and honour them. I will reward them with long life; I will save them."'

PAUL AND FIONA'S PRAYER

Dearest, precious Father, thank you that you love each one of us so much. No matter who we are, or what we've done, no matter where we've come from, or what our background is, your love for us is unconditional. Thank you, Father, that when no one really understands how I feel, you do, because you are my defender and protector, you are my God; in you I trust. When I feel tired and weak, give me strength and energy; when I feel stressed and anxious, show me your peace and calm.

You have promised in your Word that you will never leave me or forsake me. I receive that promise; I receive your mercy, love and kindness. I receive Jesus as Lord and Saviour of my life for ever. Thank you that when I call on you in his name, you answer me and rescue me. I come, Lord, for safety; I remain in you. In Jesus's name. Amen.

21

Carol Kaye

For 21 years Carol has been a member of the famous singing trio the Kaye Sisters. They are all still very good friends, she says, and they still perform together, travelling around the world from time to time. In fact, it was not that long ago that all the travelling finally caught up with her, and she ended up in hospital. Forced to take a year off, she felt it was God's way of telling her to slow down.

Carol is not just known for her singing, though. She's also an accomplished actress. Funnily enough, her first experience of this was during one of the Kaye Sisters concerts, when she was left on stage while the other two had problems with a quick change. For 20 minutes Carol kept the audience amused with comedy patter, until finally Sheila and Shan returned.

Like any actress, Carol often undergoes character changes. Carol loves the challenge of a new image, whether it's as

Miriam Ransome, the pottery-stall holder in TV's *Albion Market*, or as the attractive Maureen Slater in *Coronation Street*. In fact this was Carol's third part in that famous soap, and she fondly remembers it as one of the highlights of her acting career.

The Kaye Sisters enjoyed all the glitz and glamour of the 1950s, with many top-selling singles. Their massive chart hit 'Paper Roses' was released in 1960. They were chosen to appear in no less than three Royal Variety Performances, and were also a great success on Broadway, selling out an entire run at The Latin Quarter.

They finally split up in 1976, when Carol left the stage for the small screen. At a chance meeting in 1988 they realized that the old magic that had made them one of the top vocal groups of an era was still there, so they decided that it was time the Kaye Sisters went back on stage, and they've been there ever since.

CAROL'S FAVOURITE BIBLE VERSE

Decide today whom you will serve … As for my family and me, we will serve the Lord.

Joshua 24:15

'I have so many favourite verses highlighted in my Bible, you wouldn't believe it. It may sound strange to some people to underline or highlight verses in a Bible, but it's a great help to me. It means I can find the verse that has spoken to me much more easily, and as I look back it's a great reminder that God continues to speak to us both personally and through his Word. The verse above, however, stands out above them all.

'I am a Messianic Jew. It sounds very grand, but it simply means that I am one of God's original chosen people who has made the brilliant discovery that Jesus really was and is the Messiah. So this Old Testament verse is very personal to me, in wanting to see the rest of my family know the Lord Jesus as I know him. This has not yet happened.

'I do enjoy having my family around me: my son, my daughter-in-law and my two beautiful grandsons, Louie and Laurence. Sadly, my best friend and husband, Lenny, died very recently, and I miss him a lot. Lenny had his own variety act and was known as "The Singing Fool". He later became the Kaye Sisters' business manager.

'We are a very close, loving family, but with different religious backgrounds. My Len came from an Orthodox Jewish family. He was the youngest of seven children, and the only one who inter-married. I was from a Christian background.

After our marriage, and on my own volition, I took instruction in Judaism, and was eventually accepted into the Jewish faith at St John's Wood Progressive Synagogue in London. Our son, the actor Joe Young, was brought up in the Jewish faith and married Maria Pattinson, an actress and theatre director who came from a Catholic family. Her Grandfather was Italian. So you see, my family is a wonderful mixture of colours, just like God's family is.

'On reflection, I became Jewish not to reject Jesus but to please my husband and show respect for my newly found extended Jewish family. At that time, though, religion and God meant very little to me, because I really only lived for my family and my career in show business. With my busy schedules, I certainly didn't have the time to go to the Synagogue regularly.

'One day, something my Mother had said to me many years earlier about ignoring Jesus suddenly seemed to make sense. I realized that there was something missing in my life, and so I started reading the Holy Bible. That is, I started to read not just the Jewish Old Testament, but the New Testament as well. This, of course, would have been very much frowned upon among my circle of Jewish friends. The freedom I felt to read about Jesus, the one who claimed to be our Messiah, and the encouragement of Christian friends finally brought me home. Not only had I discovered that he was the real Messiah, but also that I could have a personal relationship with God through Jesus's death on the cross. It was wonderful, and on that day I decided that, like the verse says, I was going to serve the Lord.

'Since Len's passing, the Lord has really upheld me, comforted me and brought my family and I even closer. I still pray for them, and hope that one day they too will experience the incredible love that God has for each one of us. Until then, I lean on him.'

CAROL'S PRAYER

Dear Lord, thank you that you love families, that you have given us your family, and that you are our Heavenly Father. We pray for our families, that you will protect them, guide them, and draw them closer to you. Amen.

22

Syd Little

Syd Little is one half of the top comedy act 'Little & Large'. Starring in their own TV show which ran for many years, and receiving numerous awards for their TV, club and theatre performances throughout the country, Little & Large are now established as one of Britain's best double acts.

Syd Little was born in Blackpool, and, with his wife Sheree and their son Dominic, he has recently returned to live there again. Syd was playing guitar and singing long before his partner Eddie came on the scene. Syd enjoyed his job as a painter and decorator, and still does all his own decorating and even Eddie's! Entertaining has always been part of his life, though.

The duo have enjoyed many years at the top of their profession, but it was in 1995 that tragedy struck Syd. His eldest son Paul, from his first marriage, had become a drug user. Paul's habit had increased rapidly, and he had often pressurized his father into lending him money, which he then went and spent on drugs. On this occasion Paul had persuaded Syd to meet him outside the stage door of the Wimbledon Theatre in London, where Syd was performing in pantomime. As Syd handed the money over to his son, he was unaware that a tabloid newspaper reporter and photographer were sitting in a nearby car. Next day Syd's photo was splashed across all the newspapers, and he was being publicly accused of encouraging his son's bad habit.

Syd was devastated. Worst of all, he realized at once that he had been tricked by his own son. Under the influence of his terrible addiction, he had made even more money by setting up the story for the press. Soon afterwards Syd lost contact with Paul. Later an unexpected telephone call informed him that his son had been found dead. Paul had made the journey to Thailand and had spent the several thousand pounds that he had gained from the press on a final drugs blow-out.

That same year, while feeling utterly lost and grief-stricken, Syd once again endured the humiliation of having his personal life blasted across the national press and television news. Syd had received yet another frightening telephone call. This time it was to inform him that his daughter, Donna, had suffered multiple stab wounds and a cut throat at the hands of an enraged boyfriend. She was being treated in the emergency department of a hospital many miles away. Racing to the hospital, Syd breathed a prayer for help.

He had always been a churchgoer, but just a Sunday Christian, going more out of duty than with a real understanding of what it was all about. Just before Paul had died, though, Syd had been visited backstage by a pastor from Christians in Entertainment. As they had prayed together in

Syd's dressing room, God had felt closer and more personal to Syd than before.

It was this sense of God's closeness that Syd needed now. He needed God's strength too, in order to cope with whatever situation was awaiting him. Arriving at the hospital, he was led to the ward where Donna lay, covered in blood, medical tubes and wires. Syd held Donna's hand and thanked God that she was still alive.

The surgeons who operated on Donna said that one of the stabs had miraculously just missed her spine, and that a neighbour who was on the scene within seconds had probably saved Donna's life by quickly stemming the flow of blood. Slowly, Donna regained her strength, and has since made a full recovery. The man who stabbed her escaped abroad, and has never been found.

Syd thanked God for his daughter's life, and was eager to know more about the God who had supported him during this traumatic time. The pastor from Christians in Entertainment continued to visit Syd. It was at the Grand Theatre, Blackpool, in 1996, during the run of the *Cannon & Ball Show*, that Syd had another chance to meet God in a new way.

Little & Large were starring at the newly created Paradise Room, a plush cabaret venue at the heart of the famous Blackpool Pleasure Beach. Christians in Entertainment had invited several comics appearing in Blackpool that summer to a Bible study in Bobby Ball's dressing room. Syd was invited and was pleased to join in. While discovering that a Bible study is not as boring as it sounds, and laughing at how the pastor was fighting to get a word in among all these comics, Syd knew in his heart that those brushes with God which he had experienced were real.

The Bible study that day was all about forgiveness. The pastor explained that no matter how good we think we are, we can never live up to God's standards and the laws he has made. The term 'sin' was used in medieval times as the word to shout if an arrow missed its target – a bit like shouting 'fore!' when playing golf. The Bible says we have all missed the target.

When we break a law in our society, we expect to pay the punishment, whether it be a fine or imprisonment. This is the same in God's law, except that, because he loves us so much, God himself offers to 'pay the fine' through the sacrifice of his Son Jesus on the cross. All we need to do is to ask God to forgive us and to take over our lives. Syd knew that the time had come to make the decision about who should be in charge of his life.

With the sound of the orchestra rehearsing in the background, Syd repeated a prayer for forgiveness, led by Bobby himself. Syd asked Jesus to come into his life that day, and was overwhelmed with a feeling of love and closeness. With both comics in tears, and with hugs all round, Syd knew that this was a day he would never forget.

Syd's walk with God continues to grow, but, like many in the world of show business, it's often very difficult for him to get to church while touring and working away from home. In the autumn of 1997 Syd made his Gospel show debut in *An Evening with Syd Little & Friends*, and his autobiography will be published by HarperCollins in 1999, telling the story of how God became Syd's best friend.

SYD'S FAVOURITE BIBLE VERSE

Respect your father and your mother; and love your neighbour as you love yourself.

Matthew 19:19

'Respect is a big word. I honestly believe that if a little more respect and love was shown by each one of us, then maybe there would be a little less hate in the world. It's also important, of course, to have respect for ourselves. Having self-respect is one way of showing God that we value the life he has given us.

'No one can be perfect, of course, and we all make our mistakes, but maybe we should sometimes try a little harder to get on with that person whom we find so difficult to cope with.

'Jesus's life was full of wonderful examples of how to show respect to others. It's amazing to think that, even though he was God's Son and had every right and opportunity to be proud, demanding, aggressive and controlling, he wasn't. He literally came down to our level, put himself in our shoes, and showed respect for human life.

'Jesus showed this respect by reminding his listeners of some of the Ten Commandments. These laws were designed by God to protect people, not to restrict them, as some people think today. Of course, showing respect does not mean allowing ourselves to be walked over. Jesus was able to put the pious religious leaders of his day in their proper places, but was never aloof and was always approachable. Jesus showed respect to women too, and was probably the first women's lib campaigner! Gently talking to women, who were generally seen then as much less important than men, Jesus would tell them they were important and equal in God's eyes. Jesus loved touching the people whom no one else would go near, and he healed as many as he could physically reach.

'He hasn't changed today, of course, and has left us the job of showing the world how much respect he has for his creation. If God respects life, so must we. In all that we say and do, let's try to do it with respect, and in his name.'

SYD'S PRAYER

Oh God, I know that sometimes it is so difficult to respect others, particularly when they show no respect towards me. Help me to be able to show your love and your respect to everyone I meet today. Amen.

23

Don Maclean

Presenting BBC Radio 2's religious flagship programme may seem glamorous, but having to get up in the early hours of Sunday morning to get to the studio brings it all back down to earth! It's particularly hard when you only got to bed at 2 a.m. the night before. 'At least on radio they can't see the bags under your eyes,' smiles Don Maclean, one of the BBC's finest radio presenters. He has every right to smile, of course. His programme *Good Morning Sunday* now attracts well over two million people each week.

Presenting *Good Morning Sunday* doesn't mean that Don is always trapped in the studio, however. Some of the most memorable programmes have come from locations around the world. One programme was transmitted live from the Remembrance Day celebrations in France, and another was recorded at Bethlehem one Christmas. For Don the most moving location was Hiroshima, where the memorial service for the fiftieth anniversary of the dropping of the atomic bomb was held. It was attended by several of the survivors.

Don is very much at ease in any situation that he finds himself in, and he attributes much of this to his deep faith. He is concerned to be fully professional, but fully Christian too. He says it's not always easy to achieve both at the same time, but he tries!

Good Morning Sunday apart, Don is one of Britain's leading television and cabaret performers. He first came to the public's attention through his appearances on the BBC's *Black and White Minstrel Show*, which he hosted for three years on television and for five years on stage. He has starred in six Royal Command Performances and has appeared in 28 pantomimes, several of which he wrote and directed.

He is a keen squash player, and has won the British Celebrity Championships two years running. Don is also an experienced pilot, and flies his own aircraft regularly. Sometimes this can be very handy. Recently he was in summer season on the South Coast, and used the plane to get back to London for the radio programme each weekend.

Don is proud of the fact that, despite being surrounded by many show-biz marriages that fail, he has been married to his wife, Toni, for 30 years. His biography, *Smiling Through*, was published in 1996.

DON'S FAVOURITE BIBLE VERSE

The Lord is my light and my salvation;
I will fear no one.
The Lord protects me from all danger;
I will never be afraid.

Psalm 27:1

'If I'm asked to sum up what being a Christian means to me, I say it's about never being afraid.

'We live in a world that sometimes seems intent on scaring us. We can purchase an insurance policy for almost any eventuality these days, and we can even have insurance policies to protect claims on our insurance policies!

'We have all been enveloped by fear at one time or another, and this has the effect of making us a prisoner. The little boy who is afraid of the dark is too scared to go out of his room at night, so he stays where he is. Fear can cause us to freeze up and stop us doing what we want to do.

'I know that God is always on the lookout for me, and if I pray in times of strife or danger he will be right there for me. My faith in God's ability to protect me, and the opportunity to bring my fears before him in prayer, are the key antidotes to fear.

'What are you afraid of? Rejection? Sickness? Uncertainty? Death? We can't overcome fear just by ignoring it, but we can overcome our fears with God's help. As we hand over our fears to him, we will sense that the "light of his salvation" can extinguish the darkness of fear.'

DON'S PRAYER

> *Dear God, thank you for the gift of faith – faith to know that I can trust you to uphold me when I feel fear trying to overwhelm me. Lord, please give me the faith I had as a small child, faith that is uncluttered and simply enables me to believe in you and all your works. Amen.*

24

Ian McCaskill

Is it true that the British always talk about the weather? Is this because it changes so much, or is it because we, as a nation, are so reserved that we never know how to start a conversation any other way?

Whatever the reason, we love to know whether it's going to rain or shine, and we sit amazed while weather maps, hot spots, temperature gauges and wind speeds are explained to us by one of the television weather presenters.

One such presenter is Ian McCaskill. Born in Glasgow, he studied Science at the city's university. He now lives near Beaconsfield in Buckinghamshire and has two daughters, Victoria and Kirsty.

He's a fellow of the Royal Meteorological Society too. 'Meteorological' is a word that most of us have great trouble in pronouncing. 'Meteorologist' is even harder to say, but Ian has been one of these since 1959 when he left national service with the RAF. He joined the London Weather Centre in 1978, and has been enthralling us with his weather demonstrations ever since.

The BBC produces its weather broadcasts from its own studios based at the Television Centre in London. Every day a total of 54 weather broadcasts are made. At weekends there are 66 broadcasts per day!

Of course, the Bible says a lot about the weather, including the fact that it rains on good and bad people alike. Then there's the story of Noah and the flood, and the time when Jesus stood up in the boat and calmed the storm. It's all a reminder for Ian the weather man that God created the world and set the seasons in place. The same God who made this incredible world also made you and me, and Ian is thankful for that.

IAN'S FAVOURITE BIBLE VERSE

Look how the wild flowers grow: they don't work or make clothes for themselves. But I tell you that not even King Solomon with all his wealth had clothes as beautiful as one of these flowers.

Luke 12:27

'This verse is a wonderful mixture of things. It's a celebration of creation, a celebration of the beauties of nature, an exhortation to trust and obedience, but most of all it's urging us to live in and for the moment.

'We should not give too much heed to the past. It is fixed and frozen, and it is something we really can't do anything about. We should not give too much heed to the future either.

Again, this is beyond our grasp and is not to be known by us.

'We should seek to live in the moment. Living in the moment is so alien to us, though. We neurotic humans often try to avoid it deliberately, preferring to worry about the future or anguish over the past instead of savouring the sights and smells and sensations of right now, and trusting God to look after the bits we can't.'

IAN'S PRAYER

Dear Lord, thank you that through your creation you show us just how much you love us. I realize that the beautiful rose with its delicate petals and wonderful fragrance was made by the same God who made me. Help me to appreciate your gift of life this very moment, and to trust you for the rest. Amen.

25

Mary Millar

Millions of television viewers watching the BBC hit comedy *Keeping Up Appearances* have taken Rose, the bubbling sister of Hyacinth Bucket (pronounced 'Bouquet'!), to heart. Rose is always looking for Mr Right, but she always gets it wrong.

In real life, Mary Millar couldn't be further removed from the character she portrays. Mary is a committed Christian, so how can she play a part like Rose? 'I feel sorry for her, ' she explains. 'She's a very vulnerable woman and a bit mixed up, but a lot of us can relate to having been in that position. Also, as an actress I have to play many different characters.'

Mary has enjoyed a lifetime in the theatre, including *Camelot* on Broadway with Richard Burton and the West End successes *Popkiss*, *Pal Joey* and *Ann Veronica*, as well as *Follies* (the European premier) and Mrs Anna in *The King and I*.

In 1986 Mary was highly acclaimed for her creation of the role of Madame Giry in Andrew Lloyd Webber's *Phantom of the Opera*. 'It was wonderful working with the director, Hal Prince, and Michael Crawford,' she says. 'It didn't go perfectly every night, though, and there were several mishaps. In one performance everybody who made their stage entrance immediately slipped over, as the stage floor was so glossy! By the end of the first half everybody was hiding their hysterics as we tried to perform this serious drama on what seemed like an ice rink! When the interval came, the Stage Management used the old trick of washing the stage with Coca-Cola, except that they hadn't diluted it enough with water, and we spent the second half walking around as if our shoes had Velcro attached. It made a terrible noise!'

Comedy has always been a part of Mary's career. She played the funny fairy in pantomime for three years, and starred as the Fairy Godmother in *Cinderella*. She then stepped in to take over the role of the Red Queen in *Snow White* when Marti Caine was taken ill. Most recently Mary has been starring as Mrs Potts in *Beauty and the Beast*, Disney's new mega-musical at London's Dominion Theatre.

Just before joining *Phantom*, Mary had a series of experiences which started her thinking about the spiritual dimension of her life, and eventually they drew her to the realization that there was a God who really loved her. 'I was never searching for God,' she explains. 'I just wanted to get my daughter Lucy into a good local school which happened to be church based.' After she heard that prospective pupils had to be churchgoers, 'the hunt for a Sunday school began.'

Eventually Mary arrived at All Souls Church in Langham Place, not knowing what to expect. Lucy had been asking to go to Sunday school for some while, and content that her daughter was happy, Mary sat down in the main church to pass away the hour. As she sat there over the next few weeks, the fact that Christ knew and loved her personally became a reality to her, and Mary handed her life and career over to God.

'I'm never embarrassed talking about God,' Mary says, 'but I know that in my early days as a Christian I made the classic mistake of talking too much about my new-found faith, and I think some people thought I was a bit of a Bible basher. I was just enthusiastic about what I was experiencing and hearing, but these days I am more aware of what I am saying and who I am saying it to, especially when I am working.'

Not long after arriving on *Phantom* Mary felt the cold isolation that many Christians working in show business experience. 'I just needed someone to do some Bible study and pray with me,' Mary explains, 'but someone who understood the business as well.' Her daughter suggested that she should pray about it, so she did. And 'out of the blue there was a call from the Stage Door that a pastor from Christians in Entertainment was here to see me. I was amazed, and asked if there was any chance of having a Bible study on the show.'

Soon the *Phantom* Bible study was meeting weekly in Mary's dressing room, with many of the cast joining in. 'It was a wonderful answer to prayer,' Mary remembers.

In 1993 Mary was engaged on her first testimony tour, called 'A Night with the Stars', in which she sang and talked about her work and her faith. She continues to 'keep up her appearances' nationwide. Her 'Evening with Mary Millar' is in great demand and attracts many people who would not otherwise step inside a church building. Somehow they just can't imagine that 'Rose' is 'religious'. One local newspaper even ran the headline, 'Raunchy Rose to visit church!' Rose is not religious, of course, but as Mary says, 'If by playing the part of Rose I can get people to come and hear me and learn about my faith in Jesus, then I'm very happy.'

MARY'S FAVOURITE BIBLE VERSES

Examine me, O God, and know my mind;
test me, and discover my thoughts.
Find out if there is any evil in me
and guide me in the everlasting way.

Psalm 139:23–24

'There are three types of "testing" mentioned in the Bible. The first is that we should never put God to the test. For example, it would be foolish to step out into a busy road and expect God to stop all the traffic so that you don't get run over. We should never put ourselves into dangerous situations and expect God to pull us out.

'The second time the Bible talks about testing is when it says in 1 Thessalonians 5:21, "Put all things to the test." In other words, everything we hear about God should be tested against his Word, the Bible. People, including other Christians, are fallible and are subject to change. The Bible is infallible and totally dependable. I can stand on God's Word and know that it is relevant to today, and will never shift beneath my feet. It gives me total security and dependability.

'The third type of testing is seen in the verses I have chosen. "Lord, test *me*!" These verses can be seen as very scary. To ask God to put us to the test seems like opening ourselves up to complete and utter failure.

'The way we see this verse totally depends on how we view God. If we see him as a harsh, authoritarian figure who is ready to punish us, it's very worrying. If we see God as someone who created the world and then sat back and let us get on with life, then it's impossible to believe that he's even remotely interested in us. However, if you, like me, have felt the close and caring presence of a loving Heavenly Father, then to open ourselves up to his examination is a joy. We can trust that whatever he discovers in us, he will deal with in the most gentle of ways.

'When the clock we bought goes wrong, we can take it to the butcher or the baker or the candlestick-maker for repair. None of them will be able to help. But if we take the clock back to the clock-maker, we can be assured that he knows exactly how it works and what needs to be repaired.

'So too, we can try to overcome our difficulties in a myriad of different ways, but what better way than to take ourselves back to the God who made us, who holds the "blueprint" of my life, and who knows just what I need? Relax in the gentle and expert hands of God, then, knowing that you really can trust in him.

MARY'S PRAYER

Dear Lord, please examine me and test me. Help me to relax in your hands, knowing that you really care about me, my situation, my problems, my life. Show me what needs to be changed. Show me what I need to work on in my life. Show me how to become more like your Son Jesus, because I know that is your ultimate aim for my life. Amen.

Bryan Mosley

He's been the Mayor of Weatherfield twice in the country's most popular television soap of all time. *Coronation Street* continues to regularly attract in excess of 14 million viewers per episode. It all started on Friday 9 December 1960. Bryan has become one of the longest-serving members of the cast, having spent more than 35 years in the series.

Brought up in Leeds, Bryan has played many other roles in television and films, including some of the most famous monsters in *Dr Who* and a *Z-Cars* cop. He is a founder member of the Association of Fight Directors, and has performed many of his own stunts on film. Bryan also spent many years in the theatre. But it is as the lovable greengrocer Alf in *Coronation Street* that Bryan is best known.

He laughs about the number of letters he gets each week from people who believe that he really is Alf. Offers of help and even requests for him to send supplies from his greengrocer's shop brighten up what can sometimes be a laborious day. Sitting in his studio dressing room for hours, waiting to be called on set, Bryan takes time to learn the day's lines from his script. The story-lines are kept a closely guarded secret, and the filming schedules can be very demanding at times.

In contrast to the three marriages that Alf has clocked up on the series, Bryan has been married to his wife Norma for more than 40 years, and they enjoy being surrounded by their six children and many grandchildren. Marriage is an important part of their lives, and they recognize the demands that are placed on marriages these days. Believing that a marriage relationship needs a lot of time, understanding and hard work to keep it going, Norma and Bryan are supporters of the international Marriage Encounter Movement. This is an interdenominational organization concerned to encourage married couples to understand each other better.

Bryan felt that his first heart attack in 1991 was partly due to the pressure of being a huge public celebrity. He also blames himself, though, for not saying 'No' more often to the endless requests from charities to attend their functions. It was this spell in hospital, close to death's door, that highlighted Bryan's dependence on God once more. He was deeply touched by the thousands of letters he received, many of which said that people were praying for his recovery.

When Michael Aspel appeared from nowhere on the set of *Coronation Street* in November 1997, with the 'Red Book' tucked under his arm, Bryan couldn't believe it was for him. Yet the love that was shown to him on *This is Your Life* by colleagues, family and friends alike showed the esteem in which he is held. The final guest of the evening, the actress Kathy Staff (alias Nora Batty in *Last of the Summer Wine*), summed it all up when she said, 'I would like to say, as a fellow Christian, how lovely it is to work with someone so committed to their faith as Bryan. He's such a lovely, honest, genuine man, and to work with him is a pure joy.'

Holding a deep, quiet and confident faith, Bryan says that being able to pray is a crucial part of it. When faced with difficult decisions, he likes nothing better than to pray, telling God exactly what he would like, but then asking 'The Boss' what he thinks.

BRYAN'S FAVOURITE BIBLE VERSES

In the Lord's name, then ... do not continue to live like the heathen ... Instead, be kind and tender-hearted to one another, and forgive one another, as God has forgiven you through Christ.

Ephesians 4:17, 32

'It is really the whole of this passage that profoundly affected my life when I was about 17. Of course, it still does, because, amazingly enough, unlike any other book I know, the Bible is never out of date. It's relevant to our lives today. It really can be trusted as the living Word of God. The language the Bible has been printed in over the years may be different, and we've had many different translations, but fundamentally the message remains the same. Yes, you really can expect God to talk to you through his Word today if you take the time to sit down and ask him.

'Prayer is a direct line to God, and our prayers will always be answered. But God is a God of the unexpected, and the answer may not be the one we expect! Praying and listening are ways to hear what we are meant to do. Asking other

Christians when we do not understand is also part of this. Praying together is important because our Lord has said that where two or three are gathered in his name, he will be with them. What a wonderful source of hope this promise is. So let us rejoice and pray together always.

'God is never out of date either. He lives outside of time, and is not restricted as we are. More importantly for you and me, he understands exactly where we are today and how we are feeling, better than we know ourselves. It's because he understands us so well, that he can bring comfort when we are hurting, confidence when we are low and calmness when we are worried. He doesn't do all this out of duty. God loves to give, and delights to get alongside us whenever we let him.

'I have, of course, fallen in my faith many times, and still do, but this passage always reminds me that my goal is to try and live as God intends me to live. Fortunately, when we fall, God does not put us all the way back at the beginning, like some children's game. No, he picks us up and we continue our journey, but probably wiser! So, when I fall, I must not lie there in the mud feeling sorry for myself. Nor must I give in to the temptation to give up on my faith. I must carry on. I can rely on God to help me, but he has also given me the means to make my own decisions and choices. I must put in some of my own determination in striving for this goal, knowing that God will guide me when I falter.'

BRYAN'S PRAYER

Lord Jesus, I come before you, just as I am.
I am sorry for my sins; please forgive me.
In your name, and with your help, I forgive
all others for what they have done against me.
Come, Lord Jesus, cover me with your precious blood
and fill me anew with your Holy Spirit. Amen.

27

Alan Mullery

Alan's extraordinary rise to fame in the world of professional football began at the age of 15 when he left school to join Fulham FC as a ground-staff boy. One of his first jobs, apart from making the tea, was to catch the rats that ran under the terraces. Within two months he was signed up as a professional player, and five years later moved to Tottenham Hotspur for a record transfer fee of £72,500.

Becoming captain of Spurs in 1967, Alan played against Chelsea in the 1967 FA Cup Final, against Aston Villa in the 1970 Coca-Cola Cup Final and in 1972 in the UEFA Cup Final. By this time, Alan had also captained for England, notching up a total of 35 England caps.

Named 'Footballer of the Year' in 1975, Alan has since been awarded the MBE for his services to the sport. He became Manager of Brighton Football Club in 1976, and after this his services as Manager were employed by Charlton,

Crystal Palace and QPR, and he was also Director of Football for Barnet FC.

No stranger to television and radio, Alan makes regular appearances as a match commentator on all the terrestrial channels and also on Sky Sport. He is also an accomplished after-dinner speaker.

ALAN'S FAVOURITE BIBLE VERSES

I know what it is to be in need and what it is to have more than enough. I have learnt this secret, so that anywhere, at any time, I am content, whether I am full or hungry, whether I have too much or too little. I have the strength to face all conditions by the power that Christ gives me.

Philippians 4:12–13

'This verse is important to me because I have been in all of these situations at some time in my life since I became a Christian.

'When I lost my business to two very unsavoury people, I reached rock bottom, and needed someone to take me and hold me, just like a mother holds a baby when he or she cries or falls over. My wife June could not help me as she was in the same situation and needed the same as me. The only one who did that for me was Jesus.

'When I was involved in the secular world of football, I had success in every department. I had a large house with five bedrooms, three bathrooms, a swimming pool and cars in the drive. I would walk out through the back garden onto the golf course, play 18 holes, come home and have dinner with a glass of wine. Life was good, I had a lot of money in the bank and the holidays were plentiful and always luxurious. I ate the best food in the best restaurants and got the best treatment.

'I've also known what it's like to be hungry. At one time June and I did not eat for two days because we had no money. So, I've seen both sides of life. I didn't like the latter, of course, and it was very hard to go from rich to poor in a matter of months.

'When Jesus showed me whose side he was on, he sustained us both with his love and understanding. Sometimes you have to have the bad times to really appreciate the good times. For the last five years I have been trusting that God will provide for me, and he has kept me and June going in every department – our health, and all the things we need. He really has been, as the Bible says, "Jehovah Jireh" or "My Provider".

'God really lifts us every day. He is our strength, and without him we are nothing.'

ALAN'S PRAYER

Dear Lord, thank you that you are Jehovah Jireh, my Provider. Help me to trust you more and more each day. Amen.

28

Sir Cliff Richard

'Anyone who survives four decades is unique. To survive the sixties was a tough job. He survived flower-power, metal, glam rock, junk, punk, disco, technical bods, computer music, you name it. He's stayed in there. A survivor.'

So says Mickie Most on the career of one of the country's most enduring pop stars – Cliff Richard. Indeed, Cliff seems to have crossed all the musical boundaries and fashions over the years, and continues to make hit records – in fact, he has had a record in the charts for the equivalent of over 20 years!

Having worked extremely hard in the business for so long, it is an earned luxury for Cliff that he can now choose how to spend most of his time. The ambition to stage his musical *Heathcliff* was realized in 1997, and the show broke all previous box-office records for advance bookings. Longer holidays and doing more Gospel-based tours are now high on Cliff's priority list.

Cliff has never been shy about his faith, but he's never been one to force it down other people's throats either. When asked, he talks happily about the day when he became very aware that Jesus was not just some myth or legend, but a living reality. It took a lot of courage to stand up and publicly tell the world that he was a Christian, but the journey up to that point was a lot more private and lengthy.

Finding himself locked in religious arguments with colleagues in dressing rooms around the world on a regular basis, Cliff knew that he was eager to find some answers. He was rich and famous, but somehow he did not feel fulfilled, and wanted something more than show business could offer him. Christianity seemed to be an obvious place to start, but he suddenly realized that he actually knew very little about it.

The answers eventually came through his Christian friends, and before long he was attending Bible classes and occasionally going to church. Amazingly, this steady journey to faith was kept from the press, until on 16 June 1966, Cliff stood up in Earls Court at the Billy Graham Crusade meeting and simply said, 'I'm a Christian.'

The news was all over the world's papers the next day. No one in the music business or the entertainment business had ever made such a public declaration about something so personal. Not all the press were kind-hearted about the news. Some suggested that it was some sort of strategy to get media attention for a flagging career. This sort of silly speculation hurt Cliff, but he now had a new sense that God was in charge of his life, and this overcame any frustrating gossip.

His faith has deepened over the years, and as he thinks of the many Christians in today's entertainment business, he is glad that he was the first to stand up and be counted.

CLIFF'S FAVOURITE BIBLE VERSE

I have the strength to face all conditions by the power that Christ gives me.

Philippians 4:13

'Many of us who live a very public life know how easy it is for our perspectives and priorities to get badly distorted from time to time. Insecurities and fears, as well as inflated egos, can all be disruptive and deceptive influences.

'This verse from Philippians helps me keep my perspectives in line and is a constant source of encouragement when I have to face all manner of challenges and responsibilities.

'Firstly, it's God who does the enabling, and any success or achievement is thanks to his strength, not mine. And secondly, that strength is always available, so that no task is impossible.'

CLIFF'S PRAYER

Dear Lord, remind me that in my strength alone I can achieve little, but that in yours all things are possible. Thank you for that never-failing resource. Amen.

29

Jimmy Tibbs

Jimmy Tibbs is today one of the leading boxing trainers in the UK, and yet in the past he spent 10 years in prison after becoming involved in serious trouble in London's East End.

Before going to prison Jimmy had been a professional boxer, but after his release he ran a successful scrap-metal business. However, he had never lost his love of the sport, and he returned to it after being invited by the promoter Terry Lawless to help in training. Jimmy obtained his boxers training licence soon afterwards, and went on to become the man behind many of the world's best competitors. He has since trained many British, European and World Champions including Frank Bruno, Lloyd Honeygan, Michael Watson, Chris Pyatt and Nigel Benn.

Jimmy is still reluctant to talk about many aspects of his past, unless it helps to show others how important it is to him that God came into his life and changed everything.

JIMMY'S FAVOURITE BIBLE VERSE

Physical exercise has some value, but spiritual exercise is valuable in every way, because it promises life both for the present and for the future.

1 Timothy 4:8

'When I was about two years old as a Christian I gave my testimony in a church in the West Midlands. The Lord really blessed me, and lots of people met God. But at the same time my family and I were going through a very tough time.

'My son's wife had given birth to a Down's-syndrome boy and all the family were shocked. It was a very difficult thing to go and talk about my faith when this had just happened, but it was my son who finally persuaded me to go.

'Needless to say, there was a lot of prayer going on for my family at that time, from all the Christians who knew and loved us. But the most important lesson for me at the time was how to be obedient to the Lord. Because I was obedient in this seemingly impossible task, God really did bless me and all the family. There was a real sense that God took all our burdens away, and we felt so much at peace about everything. That little boy has grown into a lovely young lad now, and he is the apple of our eyes.

JIMMY'S PRAYER

Dear God, please help me to try and be obedient in all that you ask me to do. I know that in being obedient to you, you will bless me so that I can also bless others. Amen.

30

Sal Solo

Ever since the Beatles era, British bands have set the trends in pop music throughout the world. The seventies brought forth Led Zeppelin and Genesis, followed by punk. Then in the eighties the new bands of the day included Spandau Ballet, Duran Duran and Classix Nouveaux. Sal Solo was lead singer, songwriter and producer of most of the hits from Classix, a band who toured in 30 countries, often with audiences of 10,000 or more. They achieved number-one hits in places as diverse as Poland, Israel, Portugal and Bolivia!

All this changed in 1983 when, having completed the third Classix album, Sal embraced a personal Christian faith, after visiting San Damiano, a shrine in Italy. He recognizes that you don't have to go to a certain place to find God, but he says, 'When you make a pilgrimage, you remove yourself from your normal environment, and place yourself in an atmosphere of prayer, so it's easy for God to work on you.'

Before long, Sal found himself back in the charts with 'San Damiano', a song about his conversion, and an album entitled *Heart and Soul*. At the same time he enjoyed success on the Continent with a new band called Rok-etz, who sold a million and a half albums.

For a while he successfully continued to work in the mainstream pop world, but eventually it became obvious to him that he needed to move on. He decided to concentrate on a new form of music ministry, by presenting a Christian radio show to increase public awareness of Gospel music. His brilliant musical gifts were used in new forms of 'inspirational dance' as well as in new songs to help the nation's youth in their prayer life. This led to a whole new catalogue of devotional songs which eventually became the very first Sal Solo Gospel album, *Look at Christ*. Since then, he has gone on to work with many of his Christian friends from the mainstream pop industry, often using a unique mix of acoustic sounds and computer technology.

Sal does not want to go back to being a pop star, and so in live performances he uses giant projections as a visual focus. So although you hear the voice of Sal Solo, you most definitely will end up 'looking at Christ'.

SAL'S FAVOURITE BIBLE VERSE

Be merciful to me, O God,
because of your constant love.
Because of your great mercy
wipe away my sins!

Psalm 51:1

'Once I released an album called *Through Ancient Eyes*, which was based completely on Old Testament scriptures. It includes Psalm 51, which is my favourite Psalm and contains my favourite Bible verse.

'Of course, all the Psalms were originally songs. Although we don't have the tunes any more, they are still so poetic and musical in their language that they can speak to all people, at any time.

'In old Latin Bibles, Psalm 51 was entitled "Miserere", which means "have mercy". We believe we are a just society, and justice means getting what you deserve. Mercy, however, is something quite different. It means not getting what you do deserve! When God created our world, he set his rules and laws in place for our protection, just like any civilized society has laws to obey. The problem is, we are all guilty of having broken these laws, so if we get what we really deserve, that will mean there is a price to pay.

'But Christians know that God is full of compassion and mercy, and is willing to pay the price for us, and in so doing gives us much more than we deserve. He is the God who sent his Son Jesus to take the punishment for our wrongdoings. That must be incredibly *unjust* but gloriously *merciful*!

'Many of the Psalms were written by King David, who was a shepherd boy and a musician, and an ancestor of Jesus. God called him a man after his own heart, and yet David committed adultery and murder. How can this be after God's own heart? Well, when the prophet Nathan pointed out David's sin, he immediately owned up and repented. He totally believed that God was not only just, but merciful and so wrote this beautiful song.

'I often pray using the words of this Psalm. Whenever I feel guilty or ashamed of myself, as I'm sure we all do at times, I do not ask God for justice, but for mercy.'

SAL'S PRAYER

Have mercy on me, Lord.
Wash my iniquity, cleanse me of sin,
O Miserere Mei.
My sin always in mind,
what's evil in your sight I've done against you,
O Miserere Domine.

Cleanse me, I will be clean.
Whiter than snow wash me, save me from death,
O Miserere Mei.
I'll teach them all your ways,
my mouth will speak your praise.
Open my lips,
O Miserere Domine.

Rick Wakeman

'I've been in and out of "Yes" more than Barbara Cartland has put pen to paper!' says Rick Wakeman, known to millions for his amazing keyboard skills and brilliant compositions.

Rick has enjoyed a career spanning several decades, from his earliest days as a concert pianist through to his successful solo work. His albums with the rock group 'Yes' such as *Fragile* and *Close to the Edge* are now classics, while his solo albums such as *Journey to the Centre of the Earth* and *The Six Wives of Henry the Eighth* have also been very popular. His album *The New Gospels* musically traced the life of Jesus.

Rick is well known for his love of golf and his outrageous sense of humour, yet his life has not been laughter all the way. Three marriages, a heart attack at the age of 25 and a long struggle to stardom have all taken their toll, but it was his discovery of God which was to change his life.

'Despite being baptized at 19, I pushed God further and further away, as my love of music became more and more important,' explains Rick. However, he met and fell in love with the model and singer Nina Carter, and they started looking for a church that would marry them. As a result, they started to draw closer to the God they had both abandoned many years before. They were overjoyed at being accepted by a church that received them in true Christian love. 'I was given a renewed faith in the Church that had been lacking for more than 15 years,' recalls Rick.

The journey back to God had begun. One night, while on tour in Sydney, Australia, and struggling with an alcohol problem, Rick sat on his bed and cried. 'I had never felt so low in my entire life,' he recalls, 'and I realized I had never really been in control of my life, although I thought I was.' Then a strange calmness came over the room, and he knew there was only one thing left to do. 'The decision was to put my life back into God's hands. I asked him then and there to forgive me for all that I had done and to give me the strength to start again.' Rick knew he was back in safe hands. As if confirming this, Rick received a BAFTA Award in 1997 for his services to the industry.

Nina became a Christian soon afterwards. They began to attend church together regularly, seeing their faith grow from strength to strength.

Following an extensive tour in the USA, Rick was encouraged to take his unique Gospel show, 'The Piano Tour', around the UK. Its great success has meant that many more tours have been planned. Rick enjoys nothing better than using his wonderful sense of humour and his incredible keyboard skills to illustrate how much God is now in charge of his life.

RICK'S FAVOURITE BIBLE VERSES

> *'I know, Lord, that you are all-powerful;*
> *that you can do everything you want.*
> *You ask how I dare question your wisdom*
> *when I am so very ignorant.*
> *I talked about things I did not understand,*
> *about marvels too great for me to know.*
> *You told me to listen while you spoke*
> *and to try to answer your questions.*
> *In the past I knew only what others had told me,*
> *but now I have seen you with my own eyes.*
> *So I am ashamed of all I have said*
> *and repent in dust and ashes.'*
>
> *After the Lord had finished speaking to Job, he said to*
> *Eliphaz, 'I am angry with you and your two friends, because*
> *you did not speak the truth about me, as my servant Job did.*
> *Now take seven bulls and seven rams to Job and offer them as*
> *a sacrifice for yourselves. Job will pray for you, and I will*
> *answer his prayer and not disgrace you as you deserve. You*
> *did not speak the truth about me as he did.'*

Job 42:1–8

'My favourite Bible verses are not ones that are read very often either in private or in church, except perhaps by me!

'I often think that it is ironic that the book of Job (one of the least read books in the Bible) immediately preceded Psalms, which is probably the most read book of the Bible!

'To me, the story of Job is the most relevant book of the Old Testament regarding our lives today. It is so difficult to know whether we are being tested from above or attacked from below, or indeed whether both forces are at work.

'The first eight verses of chapter 42 explain everything, in as much as God knows all the answers and understands everything. We will *never* know the answers to the unanswerable, so why waste time looking? All we need to do is put our trust in the Lord, and he will guide us through.

'To me, Job sums it all up perfectly in these verses, and it is Job who has become my soul-mate of the Bible. I know I can never have the strength of faith he showed, but it is something I aspire to, as can everybody.

'In simple terms, I don't know how to fly a plane and I don't particularly want to. However, I have every faith in the pilot and put my trust in him to get me safely to my destination. I also don't have even a millionth of God's understanding and knowledge of this world he created, or what his destiny is for us all. However, I have every faith in him as my pilot, and put my trust in him to get me to my destination along the route he has chosen for me.

'If you're unsure whether or not you're being attacked or tested, spend some time with Job, and he'll sort you out!'

RICK'S PRAYER

Dear Lord, help us to understand the limitations of our understanding. Help us to accept that in this world there are many questions which will remain unanswered. Give us peace of mind to know that you are in total control and that you alone know the purpose of everything that happens to us, both as individuals and also as part of an ever-changing and confusing world.

Teach me not to query that which you and you alone have control over. Help us to accept that you have a reason for everything that happens to us and to others, however unacceptable it may appear at the time.

We need to give you our trust completely, Lord, which is not always easy to do. It is hard sometimes for us to differentiate between attacks from the devil and tests that you send from above.

With your strength, your guidance and the knowledge of your supreme understanding, we can perhaps begin to fulfil the purpose for which you placed us on this earth. Without you, we would never understand. Amen.

Postscript

I couldn't let this book go by without adding my own favourite verse!

CHRIS'S FAVOURITE BIBLE VERSE

Let us not give up the habit of meeting together, as some are doing. Instead, let us encourage one another all the more, since you see that the Day of the Lord is coming nearer.

Hebrews 10:25

I need friends. I need people around me who love me, and people who will laugh with me, but never at me. God never intended us to be isolated. That's why he has put us in a family, and we call each other a 'brother' or 'sister' in Christ. It's a family where we must learn not to abuse one another or take each other for granted. Instead we should enjoy and appreciate one another.

We must never give up meeting with each other. If your church is boring and lacks a real sense of God's presence, then find another one, but don't just stop going to church altogether. Call some of your best friends over for a Bible study too. It doesn't have to be all 'heavily religious' and boring; it can be great fun and can have a real impact on your life together. I have led Bible studies in the most amazing places, and it's amazing what fun it can be.

When we are together, however, have you ever noticed how easy it is to slip into gossip about another person? It's easy to tear someone apart with our words. Yet can you remember how God created the world in which we live? It was through his words!

In Genesis chapter 1 the words 'God said' are repeated 11 times. Every time God said something, something fantastic came into being. 'God said, "Let there be light," and there was light ... God said, "Let the land produce vegetation" ... And it was so ... God said, "Let us make man in our image, in our likeness" ... God saw all that he had made, and it was very good' (Genesis 1:3–31 NIV).

God used his words to create, but we often use our words to destroy. We need to ask God, like James did in the Bible, to put a guard on our mouths. Even better, why not ask God to help us to use our tongues to create, to build up and to encourage? In every situation there will always be a word of truthful encouragement somewhere. Why not try and find it?

Finally, what can be more encouraging than the final words of this verse, which say that the Day of the Lord is coming? There are some days when I really feel I can't wait to leave this planet! In fact, the sense of the verse is that things will get worse and worse until Jesus does come again. We can all see evidence of that. This is why the verse says we must encourage each other all the more. I need your encouragement more each day, and you need mine. So, as we look to that moment of Jesus's return, let's put our words into practice. Encourage someone today!

CHRIS'S PRAYER

Dear Lord, I know how easy it is for me to slip into saying bad things about others. Please help me to use my words to encourage, not to destroy. Amen.

Word Check

To someone who is new to Christianity it can seem that the Bible contains a lot of unfamiliar jargon. Here are some key biblical words, simply explained.

Christian

This does not just mean someone who tries to be nice to everyone and helps old ladies across the road in their spare time! Originally this word meant 'Christ follower'. Basically, a Christian is someone who realizes that there is a God who loves them, and who admits to needing God's help.

Grace

Not getting what I deserve. In other words, lots of mercy!

'Hallelujah!' or 'Alleluia!'

An old word which means 'Praise God!'

Sin

Originally a word that was shouted out to let people know that an arrow had missed its target.

Satan

An evil being who was once an angel at God's side but is now an arch enemy who likes to destroy all things made in God's image, including us. Although we often think in terms of God and the devil being in an equal fight, it's very important to remember that God is a million times more powerful than this evil being.

Trinity

In the same way that ice, steam and fog are all different, and yet are all made of water, so God is three in one – Father, Son and Holy Spirit – and is still God. These different parts of God all have different functions too.

Father

Jesus described God as 'Abba', which is a child's word meaning 'Daddy'. In other words, God is not an authoritarian Father with a stick, but has a caring, parental relationship with his creation. The problem is, like any children, we have the choice of accepting this or living life as we think best.

Holy Spirit

When we allow God to sit in the driving seat of our lives, he sends his Holy Spirit, who gives life to our own spirits, and leads the way.

Messiah

Meaning 'the Anointed One'. The Old Testament prophets had predicted the coming of a King, but the Jews of Jesus's time believed that God would send someone to defeat their conquerors, the Romans. But God's Messiah was totally different to what they had expected. Jesus was a 'servant King', one who was willing to die for all humanity and then become the King of people's hearts and lives, securing a place in eternity for those who believed in him.

Jesus

Jesus is most people's idea of a hero, and yet he claims to be God's Son.

Hell

Hell is basically where God isn't. If you take away all the goodness that God has put into our world, you are left with the chasm of darkness, death and destruction. This is hell.

Heaven

Because I'm in show business, I often think of our time here on earth as a 'dress rehearsal' for heaven. This is our chance to get in tune with God, become more like his Son Jesus and be prepared for the biggest banquet of them all!

Someone once described hell as a huge dining hall where all the food is placed in front of each person. Unfortunately, because the spoons they have are so enormous, they can't reach their own mouths and eventually die of starvation. In heaven, they have the same bowls and spoons, but they have learned to feed one another.

I can look forward to an incredible quality of life after death, in the presence of God, my loving heavenly Father.

CHRISTIANS IN ENTERTAINMENT

Show business has been my life, passed on through my parents, and I have enjoyed working on many of the country's best-known theatre and television shows over the years. It is because I can see the importance of communication that I have a heart for those who work in show biz.

Being on tour nine months of the year, and being away from family and friends can put an enormous strain on you, the result of which we often see reported in our daily newspapers. It's a business where you can often find yourself working in isolation, and this includes spiritual isolation. The chances of being able to find out who God is and to explore Christianity for yourself are very rare, and this is why Christians in Entertainment exists.

Founded in 1982, CIE has become a lifeline to many in the world of show business as we seek to support, encourage and pray for those in our industry.

For more information contact Christians in Entertainment
PO Box 17205
London
SE26 4ZL
Tel: 01737 550375
E:mail: ChrisGidney@compuserve.com
Web page: http://ourworld.compuserve.com/homepages/
chrisgidney